FREDERICKSON'S

History of the
ANN ARBOR
AUTO AND TRAIN
FERRIES

Complete with Pictures

Arthur C. and Lucy F. Frederickson

FREDERICKSON'S HISTORY OF THE ANN ARBOR AUTO and TRAIN FERRIES

Complete with Pictures

By Arthur C. and Lucy F. Frederickson

Published by:

Gulls Nest Publishing
P. O. Box 272
Frankfort, MI   49635-0272

ISBN   0-9641173-0-4 $9.95

Printed by Patterson Printing, Benton Harbor, MI

Carl F. Frederickson

To our son Carl, the third
generation of Frederickson's to
sail on the Ann Arbor
Carferries.

The carferries came and during their brief stay did so much to develop our present system of transportation, then were so easily forgotten after they had gone.

The facts in this history of the Ann Arbor carferries were copied from the very brief notations in the many log books. The stories built around these facts were furnished by the known seafaring men who were present at these times. As many of these men have long since passed on,parts of this history came from twice-told tales and at times may vary slightly from the truth.

A.C.F.

The Kewaunee Enterprise

KEWAUNEE, WIS., FRIDAY, DECEMBER 2, 1892

THE ANN ARBOR NO. 1.
The Monster Ferry Boat in Which Freight Trains will be Transported Across Old Lake Michigan

ARRIVES AT KEWAUNEE

History A Notable Event in the of Lake Commerce and Ship Building

HISTORY of HER CONSTRUCTION

Sunday, Nov. 27 marked an epoch not only in the history of Kewaunee, but in that of the whole country, and is the most notable event of the generation in the annals of lake navigation. On that day a train of loaded cars was successfully transferred bodily sixty miles across an open and stormy body of water. Saturday afternoon, after much straining of eye-sight and many slighting remarks by the incredulous, smoke was discerned in the direction of Frankfort and within an hour the monster leviathan car-ferry steamer Ann

Arbor No. 1 without a flag flying or a whistle blowing, and without as much commotion as is made by a tug steamed majestically into the harbor and backed into the slip prepared for her, as if the business had been for every day occurrence for her for years. So quietly had she stolen in that only a few people of the city were aware of her plight and word of it spread. Work on the apron in the slip to the boat was at once commenced. Some slight changes in the structure were found necessary, and it was seven o'clock Sunday evening before the work of loading her with cars began. She was loaded in about half an hour the cars running smoothly into the boat and only sinking her to a depth of about two feet, making her draw about eleven feet and four inches when loaded. She cleared for Frankfort about eleven o'clock Sunday evening and made the run smoothly in about six hours. Her first load consisted of twenty-two cars loaded with flour from the Pillsbury mills at Minneapolis, destined for England, Ireland and Scotland.

1

The problem of ferrying cars across Lake Michigan originated in the brilliant mind of Gov. James M. Ashley over 15 years ago. When he built the Toledo, Ann Arbor and North Michigan railroad he had it in his mind, and it never got away from him, Nor ever did he abandon for a single moment the belief that the day would come when boats would be built to carry loaded freight cars across Lake Michigan. Many of the greatest railroad men in the country listened to Gov. Ashley's pan, but they had very little confidence in the successful outcome of such a project. Six years ago

GOVERNOR ASHLEY WAS
READY

And willing to try the experiment of crossing Lake Michigan with a train of loaded cars, but the capitalists of the country shook their heads at his bold and daring project. They gave him credit for boldness and originality, but were not willing to stake their money on the outcome of such a hazardous undertaking, as they called it.

Then year ago when Governor Ashley made the statement before a gathering of railroad magnates in New York city, that whole trains of cars would be

CARRIED ACROSS LAKE
MICHIGAN

With as much ease as they were being ferried across the Detroit river from Windsor to Detroit, the party almost laughed in his face, and plainly told him the day for the consummation of such a project would never come.

Governor Ashley was not then in a position to carry out his original ideas. He did not have a road built to the shores of Lake Michigan and was not able to make satisfactory arrangements with other roads west of Lake Michigan, to enter into traffic arrangements with his line. He put his ideas quietly away for the time being but informed the doubting Thomases that the day would come if God spared his health, when he would be able to carry out his ideas without the assistance of any of those whom he had asked to aid him in his enterprise. Mr Ashley went to work and extended his lines in all directions throughout Michigan and improved them so that the road was placed in first class condition. He kept pushing the lines by degrees toward Lake Michigan and finally reached Copemish. Here he took a breathing spell and examined the shores of the lake to see where the best place was to make a terminus.

After a careful investigation he decided that the road should be pushed through to Frankfort.

It only required a few months to construct this extension, and then Governor Ashley stood on the east shores of Lake Michigan and looked across its blue waters and said to himself. "Well the day is near at hand when my cherished hopes of carrying trains of loaded cars across Lake Michigan will be realized."

After having served as Governor of Montana, James M. Ashley turned too high finance and began purchasing railroad stock. In 1877 he secured all the rights of the Toledo and Ann Arbor Railroad, no track had yet been laid. Some of this stock he then sold, mostly to citizens of Ann Arbor who realized the value of a railroad to their rapidly growing community.

Between November 1877 and May 1878 track was laid from Alexis, Ohio to Ann Arbor, Michigan. The freight train entered Ann Arbor June 21st and first passenger train several days later. Governor Ashley then purchased the five mile long Toledo and State Line R. R. From the Pennsylvania R.R. This connected with the newly built line to Ann Arbor.

Ferry Vermont one of the many operating around our harbor in the old days as seen with a full quota of happy passengers. Cruising by water before the auto, was the only way to see much of the scenery and enjoy a good rest at the same time. In the background one can see the schooner Michicott and Pottawattamie in the distance.

The locomotive was brought to Frankfort by scow and the tug Erma Wheeler from Manistee and unloaded near the foot of Eighth Street. It was then used in the building of the Frankfort and South Eastern Railway until it was completed to Copemish in 1889.

As Governor Ashley continued to extend his railroad further north he envisioned of a route across Lake Michigan ferrying freight cars, such as was being done on the Detroit River or Straits. He contended that ships could easily cross the lake and in time might be built to cross the oceans, capable of carrying whole trains. First acclaimed and then scoffed at by other financiers he worked toward his goal, to prove that the cheapest and fastest way to the northwest was shipping it by boxcars aboard a ship, not in unloading the freight and putting it aboard a package freighter.

In 1887 the railroad was open for traffic as far north as Cadillac and in 1889 to Copemish. Governor Ashley was looking for a port on Lake Michigan suitable for a terminus for his projected carferry fleet. After checking several Lake Michigan ports he decided on the Frankfort Harbor. He then purchased the Frankfort and South Eastern R. R. In 1892. This road had been built several years earlier by interested citizens of Frankfort and South Frankfort.

The first package freight boats on the run from Frankfort to Kewaunee, Wisconsin, were the Steamers Osceola, City of Marquette and the Alice Stafford. The Osceola was built in Bay City in 1882. It was 193 feet long, with a 34-foot beam and of 980 tons.

Osceola

The Osceola was owned by the Delaware and Lackawana System of which the T.A.A. and N.M. Railroad constituted a portion. When she arrived here the Woodward unloading dock was still under construction as the dock crew had been on a strike for higher wages. This delayed her departure until January 12th. On her first trip the Osceola as an experiment only took about half a cargo, 5,500 barrels of flour--her full capacity being 10,000 barrels.

The Osceola while unloading in Frankfort on January 14, 1892, burst a steam pipe, which caused the death of her 1st assistant engineer.

The Osceola during 1892, after March 20th was carrying

35 to 40 carloads of flour per trip, making one round trip every 24 hours.

This freight had to be shipped in box cars alongside the warehouse, unloaded, hauled through the warehouse, loaded into the boats, taken across the lake, unloaded and packed again into box cars at the other end of the line. This process was slow and expensive, requiring large forces of labor on both shores. At this time it cost 40¢ per ton to handle the contents of the average car or from $6 to $12 per car from car to boat, compared with $2 cost per car to place the entire car and its contents aboard a carferry. It was this expense of handling the broken bulk freight and the time saved enroute across the lake instead of the long way around by Chicago that gave Governor Ashley the idea of just how much money could be made by building a ship able to carry a trainload of box cars across the lake without having to handle their contents twice enroute.

The City of Marquette

The City of Marquette was built in Manitowoc, Wisconsin, in 1890 and of 341 gross tons. She was purchased by the T.A.A.

& N. M. in April 1892 and sold by them in 1893. During her long life she was owned or leased by almost every steamship company on Lake Michigan. She was condemned about 1929 and taken to Escanaba where she was built into a barge in 1930. She was bought by Charles McDonald of Washington Island who used her in Jackson harbor. In 1930 she was purchased by Jack Lyons of Whitehall, Michigan. He renamed her Aching Hearts. She was used as a cement mixer while he was building the new docks at Mackinaw City for the State Highway Department. Later that year, full of green cement, she rolled over and sank. She was then towed out into the Straits and laid to rest near New Shoal Number 3. During 1892 the City of Marquette made 71 round trips from Kewaunee to Frankfort--a total of 10,000 miles.

Schooner Ative,small two master. She missed the harbor piers in a northwest sea and fog making the beach broadside and stripped off her canvas. Flying light she came in close, enabling the crew to get ashore and later transport goods ashore as seen in the picture.

Schooner loaded at Crane Mill in Elberta. Notice difference of fore and aft loaded by rake of spars

The Alice Stafford, formerly the Str. Lora, was built in Benton Harbor in 1882 and was of 859 gross tons.

Early picture of West end of Frankfort harbor taken from south side before the railroad came. It shows sthe original river opening on the north side of the island

One of the first sawmills built by Banks. It burned in 1875. The two loaded schooners LaPetite and Emma Thompson are awaiting weather

The Ann Arbor Railroad purchased the Tug G.B. Doane on August 5, 1892, to be used to break up the ice in Frankfort harbor and assist the carferries in winding around into the slip. She was stationed here and placed in command of Capt. Waters with Nels Holms as her Chief Engineer. Before carferries arrived, she was used as a passenger ferry for crossing the river and assisted in building the dock and slip. The Captain also used to pick up a tow now and then, as there were lots of schooners flying the old flag for assistance of a tug in the days of wooden ships and iron men.

Tug Doane

The Tug Doane proved too small for this work so they tied her up that fall at the Furnace Dock in Elberta and chartered the tug Saugatuck. The next spring when the ice went out the old Doane sank. Some outside men came here and after pumping her out bought her for a song and took her away.

Frankfort Harbor 1889. Two schooners, the Driver and the Fearless lumber laden are outward bound. On the left is the wooded "Island" where the Johnson, Robertson and Penfold fish shanties, nets and docks can be seen. The lighthouse tender Dahlia is tied to the dock on the north side. Next to her on the right can be seen the stern of the Mary Mills in the slip at the newly completed F. & S. E. Railway dock and warehouse. Back of the tree is the steam and sail yacht Florence.

The Saugatuck was a nice large roomy tug and was operated by Captain Rhyrsese and his two sons. She hailed out of Grand Haven and arrived in our harbor on November 24, 1892.

The Steamer Ann Arbor Number 1 was built at the Craig ship yards in Toledo, Ohio. Her keel was laid with a big celebration on June 10, 1892, and she was launched September 29th of the same year.

One of the outstanding features of the Ann Arbor Number 1 was that she was the first triple screw boat ever used in this country. She had one at the bow and one on each quarter. The bow was designed to run up on the ice and break it with the weight of the vessel, and to this end had a very rank sheer extending down to the screw itself. Her general dimensions were 267 feet long overall, 52 foot beam. Her hull was very solid and outside planking on her bow was 5 inch oak, sheathed four feet above and below the water line with 3-16" steel plate.

The engines were three sets of compounds having cylinders 20"x40" over 36"; two stern and one in the bow. They had independent condensers and could be worked at high pressure if occasion demanded. There were also three fire box boilers, worked at 125 pounds per square inch. Two supplied the after engines and one was in the bow, but all three could be connected with the after engines if desired. Cards from the engines showed 610 h.p. when making 86 revolutions per minutes.

She was built to carry 24 cars(which were smaller than those of today), and when she first came out she made about 14 miles per hour. She was of 1,128 gross tons and her loaded draft was about 11'4" aft.

It cost about $260,000 to build her.

Ann Arbor No. 1

The Ann Arbor No. 1 left Toledo November 10th passing Detroit, November 11th and arriving at Frankfort 9:00 a.m. November 16, 1892.

While people from near and far came aboard to look her over she took on supplies, fuel and shipped some new hands. The apron where she docked had to have several adjustments also.

Governor Ashley was unable to find to find shippers who were willing to trust their freight to the hazards of crossing the big lake. Finally by bringing pressure on the coal company from which the railroad purchased its fuel he was able to route four carloads via the Ann Arbor Carferries from Frankfort, Michigan, to Kewaunee, Wisconsin.

After taking on this cargo and making everything well fast she left Frankfort for Kewaunee on her first trip, with the Ashleys aboard, at 8:00 a.m. on November 24th.

When the A. A. No.1 fetched the west shore on her first loaded trip it was foggy and as everything was strange to her Master and crew, including her compass and running time she had the misfortune to pile up on the beach just north of Kewaunee. Some fish tugs heard her blowing and came alongside. Mr. Ashley asked them to notify every one of importance in the Great Lake Area, also to send for all available tugs and vessels to help pull her off. He realized that this would get in all the papers and advertise the carferries, also that he must get her off at once regardless of cost.

On the second day the Tug Favorite, owned by the Swain Wrecking Company arrived. There were so many boats around her that the Favorite had trouble getting close enough to take a tow line. Smoke from the fleet could be seen for miles and miles. The Favorite with the help of others pulled her off on the 26th after she had let go both anchors and paid out all the anchor chain to lighten herself up. She arrived in Kewaunee at 4:00 p.m. the same day with no apparent damage. Here the apron and rails also needed adjustments, etc.

At the time this information was written the fleet consisted of five large commodious luxurious ships that transport freight, passengers and autos across Lake Michigan. With year round service and irrespective of unexpected rail delays and inclement weather the maintained a very close schedule.

They operated daily from the home port of Frankfort to Manitowoc and Kewaunee, Wisconsin, and to Manistique and Menominee, Michigan. Thus, saving the traveling public and shippers several hundreds of delayed miles through the ever increasing congested area around the lake.

This new carferry operation cut down the cost of package freight transportation and the smaller freight and passenger boats in this area were soon looking elsewhere for cargoes.

Entrance to Frankfort Harbor about 1890. The life-saving station on the left was built in 1887. The light on the end of the pier was established in 1873. Rodal's fishing boat the Queen is drying her sails at the dock. The west carferry slip was built near the tree iin the foreground.

The old Bell Ferry. She carried thousands of crew members and passengers back and forth across Betsie Bay from the north side to the ferry landing in Elberta at five cents each. Shown here hauled out on dock for spring jet out and overhauling. She was called Bell Ferry, as when she was on the wrong side one would ring the large hanging bell on the dock and the ferry would come over. During the winter you could walk the ice and in summer some crew members had row boats.

Of course the taxi and autos did away with both. The original terminal of the railroad was on the North side of Betsie Bay in Frankfort. Here before the advent of the carferries freight was unloaded and transferred to package freighters for crosslake shipment.

The Ann Arbor Railroad was 292 miles long. Crossing the State of Michigan in a north westerly direction from Toledo, Ohio, to their terminal on the eastern shore of Lake Michigan, located at the twin cities of Frankfort and Elberta, Michigan.

The Steamer Ann Arbor No. 2 was the second all wood carferry built for the Toledo, Ann Arbor and Northern Railroad company by the Craig ship Yards of Toledo, Ohio. She was 264 feet long with 53 foot beam and of 1,144.91 gross tons, designed by Mr. F. E. Kirby and built along the same lines and structure as her sister ship the A. A. No. 1, at the cost of about $280,000.

Ann Arbor No. 2 on her first trip into Frankfort. Notice the square pilot house forward and open top where the captain and pilots stood their watches. Commands to the wheelsman in the lower house were passed down through a boxed in opening in the deck called a guff box. Like the A. A. No. 1 she had no after pilot house.

The A.A. No. 2 left the Toledo shipyards bound for Frankfort at 3:00 p.m. on December 24, 1892, passed Detroit Saturday, December 25. While bucking 5 inches of solid ice when crossing Lake St. Clair and in parts of the St. Clair River, she loosened some of the steel plates covering her wooden bows. This caused her to stop at the shipyards in Port Huron for repairs before starting up lake Huron for Mackinaw.

The A.A. No. 1 left Frankfort at 4:00 a.m. on January 12, 1893, just after the wind had let up during a big blow from the southward. She was bound for Kewaunee and steered into the wind until she was high enough to make a decent run after squaring away before the sea. When about two hours out of Kewaunee the wind went N.N.E. and started to blow a regular gale with snow, Captain Kelly decided to head for Manitowoc as he could get some lee from under Two River Point, and Kewaunee, then as it is today, was always bad to make in easterly weather if there are any large seas. After being several hours late she arrived in Manitowoc and laid there windbound. This was a hard trip for Boat One and she as well as her crew, was badly shaken up when she, rolled, and dove around while riding the big cross seas. They were three days making Kewaunee.

While laying in Manitowoc most of the town was down to look her over, she being the first ship of this kind ever there. This, of course, started the people and newspapers talking about carferries trading out of Manitowoc as their harbor could be entered in any weather. After this trip some of the crew didn't like bad weather and took off, and by the time Boat One had been out about two months she had shipped 29 different engineers.

In the spring of 1893 the railroad company had lots of delays with their boats while making Frankfort harbor because of the shallow water at the entrance of the piers. The boats in fear of striking bottom here hung off under the lee of the west shore during bad weather from the westward. To overcome this the railroad company upon the advice of experts decided to lay out some large pipes 1,000 feet long into the lake at the end of the piers. Whenever the seas became very large, they would force out some oil through these pipes and as it floated to the surface it would flatten out the seas. This did knock the top off the sea but left a large dead swell still running which caused the boats to rise and fall and yaw around against their rudder, sticking the bottom and often the piers. (These wooden ships were tough, could stand lots of abuse, and as there was a certain amount of give to their hulls, they seldom did much damage when they fetched up. This same treatment on a solid steel hull would keep a boat in the shipyards most of the time.)

These pipes also kept filling with sand and this experiment was soon discontinued. The idea was a good one and even to this day all ships carry their own oil tanks forward on each side (called

17

storm oil) and when running before a big sea, under check, with the oil tanks open it helps a great deal. This does not often apply to carferries as they seldom check while entering a breakwater in any seaway, but it has proved a great help to lower lakers and other classes of shops which do check down when making a harbor, giving the sea time enough to carry the oil ahead of her knocking the top off the big seas, where the power in them lies.

After the A.A. No. 1 and 2 had been in operation for about a year they decided that the forward end engines were of very little help to them. Later when the freight slacked up they took turns going to the ship yards in Toledo and had them removed. Those engines were later installed in the A. A. No. 3 when she came out new on November 20, 1898, and were used in her until she was rebuilt in 1922.

February 24, 1894, the A. a. No. 1 and City of Marquette sutck in the ice outside Frankfort.

The A.A. No. 1 and 2 fighting their way through the heavy ice at the harbor entrance about 1894.

Heading for Frankfort. The A.A. No. 1 on the right, the Pottawattamie towing the schooner Senator and the tug Hannah Sullivan towing the Minnehaha about 1894.

Looking up one of the five such slips in Manistique harbor in about 1894. Taken from near carferry slip. These slips were owned by the Chicago Lumber and Manistique Lumber Company. Schooners and lumber barges came into slip alongside of the limber piles and loaded. Notice small schooner in the foreground unloaded, brought salt for fishermen also wooden tram on ramp that conveyed hand cart of lumber for piling on the left and right from mill.

When the A.A. No. 1 and 2 were first built the overhead and ship's sides extended so far aft on the car deck that there was very little clearance for the box cars.

As time went on the owners, at the suggestions of the crew, tried to improve these conditions because of the damage done to the cargo during loading and unloading of the boats.

To overcome this they cut down the ship's sides and the overhead for a distance of about one and a half freight car lengths or 50 feet. This left the stern well open but with very little protection from the weather. At first they left a part of her overhead forming a narrow fore and aft walk in the very center of the ship for the Captain to stand on while backing around in port. Later they removed this also and the Captain had to stand way aft on top of a box car with a line in each had attached to the port and starboard engine whistles while backing into a dock. Handling the lines like driving a team of horses towing barges through the old Erie canal and usually swearing as much, particularly while standing out there in the open during 30 below zero weather or a bad rain squall.

Ann Arbor No. 1 tied up outside the slip and heading east. This was early in her life before it was found necessary to cut down her sides aft as larger box cars began hitting her sides and overhead. The large windows in her sides were later replaced with portholes. The extra smoke stack was for her forward engine.

Annarbor Car Ferry No. 1. This boat was the first of a large fleet of car ferries that now ply the open waters on the Great Lakes

Ann Arbor No. 1 showing her cut down side and forward stack removed. This was taken in Kewaunee and shows the life-saving station at her bow. This building was sold when the station was deactivated.

In the early days of carferries plying in and out of Manistique, Michigan, they found the dredged harbor often so full of drifting sawdust, partly submerged by the current from the many sawmills located upstream that at times it was a very slow process for the boats to wind around and tie up to the dock. There were times when so much sawdust came floating down stream that it jammed up at the harbor entrance and piled up form behind so high that it completely covered the sea wall, forcing the lower part to the bottom where some of it still rests.

To shorten this delay in parking their boats the railroad company leased the Tug Gifford from the Chicago Lumber Company to assist the boats in and out of the harbor. This tug was kept in Manistique and was operated by Captain Eli Garrett. The Tug Gifford was later sold to Mr. A. M. Shesburgh, who was one of the founders of Thompson, Michigan.

The Ann Arbor No. 1 about 1895. Her sides are partially cut away and her lifeboats have been moved forward. Str. John Dewar and Petoskey on north side of harbor.

The A. A. No. 2 about 1895, in the slip in the foreground. Life-saving station on left. "Island" in center background.

Tug E. D. Holton purchased and rebuilt by Dr. A. J. Slyfield and his sons of Frankfort in 1895-96 at the Frankfort ship yard.

The tug Holton after being rebuilt was often used by the Ann Arbor Railroad to break ice and as a ferry across the bay. Burned at Dollar Bay 1927.

Steamer J. C Ford also leased by the Ann Arbor during the winter months. Carried barrels of flour, often carried salt from Manistee. Chartered to run with George Farwell 1896 to Frankfort, Manitowoc and Kewaunee.

A.A. No.2 and in the background on the north side can be seen the tent where William Jennings Bryan made his speech in 1896 for 16 to 1 free silver. Schooners awaiting lumber at the docks. Butler mill at foot of Seventh St. at right. Yacht Florence in harbor.

During January and February 1897, the A. A. No. 1 and 2 were stuck fast in the windrowed ice for 23 days between Arcadia and Manistee about seven miles offshore. Before the A. A. No. 2 became stuck and while working the ice she broke the key in her rudder stock. This, of course, set her rudder adrift making it useless. The Chief Engineer walked the seven miles ashore then down the beach to Manistee. Here Mr. Tom Ray founder of the Manistee Iron Works helped him make a new key. The Chief after finding refreshments and a good night's lodging, ordered fuel and supplies sent out the next day. These supplies had to be hauled out with horses and sleighs. The Chief rode out with them, but it was a long slow ride as the men had to chop a road through numerous windrows of ice with iron bars and axes.

After a good stiff breeze of wind from the eastward which released the pressure off the ice the boats worked themselves loose and went back into operation again with very little damage from this ice jam.

The Ann Arbor Number 3 was the first all steel carferry of

our fleet

She was built in Cleveland by the Globe Iron Works and left there on her maiden voyage at 6:55 a.m. November 20, 1898, bound for her home port of Frankfort, with Captain W.P. Robertson and Chief Engineer Tom Cosgrove in charge of her. She ran into a bad snow storm out of the N.W. coming up Lake Huron and dropped her hook at Mackinaw overnight, arriving in Frankfort at 3:29 a.m. on November 24th. After taking on fuel, supplies and cargo she left Frankfort bound for Kewaunee with her first load of cars on November 28th, making this run from pier to pier in five hours and seven minutes.

When the A. A. No. 3 first came out she had the two horizontal engines that came out of the forward ends of the A. A. No.s 1 and 2. She was 258 feet long and of 58 foot beam, and had two smoke stacks and four boilers.

She was the only one of our ships with a waterbottom (or two bottom). Perhaps this is why she has led such a charmed life and has only been on the bottom once (outside) in her many years at sea.

Early in her life she had two cabins on her spar deck and between these she had a grain hatch so arranged that while she was in the slip at Frankfort exchanging her regular cargoes of freight cars, the leg from the grain elevator (that stood just south of the present west slip) could be lowered into this hatch to unload her grain cargo without causing any delay to the freight trains.

The A. A. No. 3 loaded this grain at Manitowoc, Wisconsin, and carried besides her regular cargo of freight cars, average cargoes of grain in her hold of 20,000 bushels of wheat, 20,000 bushels of oats, 22,000 bushels of rye, and 21,000 bushels of corn.

She also carried package freight from Manistique, Michigan, to Frankfort years ago (thus the large gangways in her sides). While in this trade there were times when she was loaded so heavily that they almost lost her, during unexpected heavy weather.

The A. A. No. 3 has visited many Great Lakes ports and while seeking shelter from a bad blow in the old days has dropped her hook in many places that are almost forgotten today.

There were times during bad weather that she, like many others, when way overdue, was given up for lost, and during her lifetime she had pounded her proud bows through many a bad blow or "gagger" as old Captain O.B. Olsen, with his corn cob pipe, shuffling overshoes and rope yarn belt around his middle, used to say. With the passing of this grand old man and many others that most broken heartedly were forced, with the ever increasing smokestacks appearing on the horizon, to change over from sail to steam, went much unwritten, very interesting history of Lake Michigan. From the days of the mighty Mormon King, James Jesse Strang of the Beavers and Captain Roaring Dan Seavy, the Lake Michigan Pirate, with his big hearted, two fisted Mate Ed Ward, aboard their schooner Wanderer, to the late King Ben Parnel and Queen Mary of Benton Harbor whose ships the Rising Sun and Rosebelle, enroute to the King's summer home on High Isle hove to in our fair harbor and have long since gone.

In the early days of carferries they used to stop and pick up passengers at almost any place they could tie up. the Hotel Dock in Frankfort, City Dock in Manistique and Escanaba, Mason's Dock in Gladstone, Michigan (they traded here as early as 1897) eleven foot Shoal Lightship, Sturgeon Bay bridge and canal, also the dock below the bridge at Menominee, Michigan, and may other out of the way places.

The A. A. No. 3 entering Frankfort shortly after she came out. This shows the cat-walk going out to the light on the end of the pier. Notice her two stalwart ship stacks and no after pilot house.

Taken from the 8th Street Bridge looking east down Manitowocc River in about the fall of 1898. One can see double smoke stacks of carferries in C.N.W. slip at the lake front. Most of these ships are awaiting their turn to be tugged up river for winter lay up. This narrowing of the channel made navigation hazardous to carferries trading up and down the Soo Slip.

February 15, 1899, the A. A. No. 3 inbound, A. A. No. 2 and Alice Stafford outbound. Notice the ladder from stern of the A. A. No. 3 to ice also open gangway inside. This was for the crew to get on and off the ice in trying to free her. Canvas rolled up on the after deck used for enclosing stern in bad weather.

View of Frankfort harbor showing the package freight boats. The first on the left was the City of Fremont with the tug Saugatuck alongside. Next are the George Farwell and Hennepin. The A. A. No. 1 is in the slip and the A. A. No. 2 is going out through the piers. This was taken about 1899 after the freight sheds had been moved to the south side of the bay.

Schooner Wanderer inbound Frankfort about 1900. First owned by Banister and later by Capt. Dan Seavy.

On February 2, 1899 the A. A. No. 1 left Frankfort bound for Menominee with Capt. Frank Butler as her Master. She became stuck fast in the heavy ice just past Sherwood point in Green Bay, Wisconsin, on February 3rd and was 63 days getting back home. The Ann Arbor Railroad hired the Str. Algoma to break her loose and assist her, but they both broke buckets off their wheels and laid there side by side until spring. Supplies and fuel had to be hauled out from Sturgeon Bay with horses and sleighs.

Looking down bound Manitowocc River in about 1900. On the left one can see facing of present Soo Slip. The crossing 10th and 8th Street bridges. Notice Goodrich passenger boat at their dock near harbor entrance on left and no lighthouse on south breakwater. The bridge tenders at this time swung them open after releasing the lock or stops by leaning their weight on long wooden handles.

During May in 1900, while the A. A. No. 1 was backing around into the Wisconsin central Slip (now known as the Soo Line), the lookout on watch knocked all the clamps off the port center track. The jar of the boat bumping against the dock started this string of cars running aft. When the trucks from the after car fell over the stern of the boat, the end of the car dropped down onto the deck and acting as a drag or brake caused the string of cars to stop running. They had to let her lay there at anchor until a diver went down and made a line fast on the trucks so that they could hoist them aboard where the string of cars was hove back up the track, the car raised up and the trucks put back in place.

The A. A. No. 1 and 3. The grain hatch can be seen between the No. 3's split cabin. Fairchild's fish tug Maggie Lutz in the foreground. Mackinaw boat to her right owned by Rubier Fish Co.

Building of the famous Royal Frontenac Hotel by the Ann Arbor Railroad. Once a show place of northern Michigan. Completed in 1900 and burned in January 1912.

The A. A. No. 1 left Frankfort at 8 p.m. on January 7, 1901, bound for Manistique. She had a good run northbound and after exchanging cargoes there she departed at 5:30 a.m. January 8th, homeward bound. When down near Port aux Barques, about one hour out, it started to blow a regular living gale from the south and it turned very cold. The A. A. No. 1 had lost a couple of buckets off her port propeller the trip before in the heavy ice in Green Bay. Also, her steering gear had lots of play and was not in very good shape at this time. The A. A. No. 1 had been on the go most of the time since she came out, and, as the freight was increasing as this short cut across the lake became better known, the company didn't take time to lay their boats up long enough for repairs. The suction pipes in her hold were rusted badly. This made it very hard to pump the water out of her hull unless she was loaded well by the stern and in a big seaway this was not considered proper distribution of cargo. At the bottom of each bulkhead there were holes cut(called limbers) for the water to run aft to be pumped out. Chains were threaded through these holes so that the lookout could give them a pull now and then to make sure the limbers were clean of dirt so the water could run free. They being well rusted often parted. With things in this condition the A. A. No. 1 was not in the best of shape to combat the big seas on this trip. She started making water that all ran forward causing her to gradually tip by the head.

As the seas became bigger they crept up on her stern making ice. This extra weight on her stern and the extra water in her holds made conditions look very bad. The cars in the port center started running fore and aft as the gear became loose. The crew blocked the tracks and caused some of these cars to jump onto the wooden deck, where the wheels of the cars went through, forming a brake that stopped them running. There were no lights between decks and everyone carried their own lantern. They had windows instead of portholes in her sides. In spite of all this, the A. A. No. 1 got down in the lee of the land close in, south of Frankfort. Then the quadrant became loose and the key jumped

34

out on the rudder stock and they had to steer her with the engines until they broke out all hands, chopped the ice off her stern and connected the emergency gear on the tiller aft. She made Frankfort then after 38 hours in the lake, although she was so full of water and ice that 'tis very doubtful if she could have kept her noble head up for another five miles.

A. A. No. 2 in slip with leg from elevator unloading grain. On the right can be seen the wind blown remains of the Royal Frontenac Hotel. She was partially built when she collapsed in 1901. Small building on right was emergency boat house of the Life-saving service. Ann Arbor office is in the foreground.

A. A. No. 1 stuck fast on the bottom inside the piers. Often in the early days of carferrying ships entering the harbor became stuck on the sandbar in the harbor entrance A. A. No. 1 was in this picture. This shows the No. 3 backed down to her stern to stern and after lining up the rails with the power of stern cable winches part of Boat 1's cargo was removed lightening her enough so she could move.

The A. A. No. 3 lightening the A. A. No. 1.

On July 30, 1902 the A. A. No. 3 stopped between the piers in Frankfort to take some passengers off the Northbound Steamer Charlevoix that were bound for Manitowoc. (This steamer Charlevoix was the former Champlain, that burned outside of Charlevoix with a great loss of life, was later rebuilt and renamed the Kansas and burned to a total loss at Manistee in 1920).

The A. A. No. 1 outbound from Frankfort in 1903. Frozen fast in the ice at the harbor entrance. Hired shore hands can be seen spuding and sawing the ice into cakes. It was then hauled out with teams of horses in an effort to free the imprisoned ship. Sometimes this worked other times it was necessary to wait for a shift of the wind. The Royal Frontenac Hotel can be seen under her stern.

Looking west over Betsie Bay, Frankfort Harbor in about 1903. The Bellows sawmill in the foreground with logs in booms afloat in the river. Notice size of Royal Frontenac Hotel at west end of bay and the A. A. No. 1 and 2 at docks near elevator at harbor entrance. This elevator was also built by the Ann Arbor Railroad.

During 1903 while Capt. B. F. Tulledge was Master of the A. A. No. 1 and D.H. Woods was her Chief Engineer she left Frankfort at 6 a.m. on May 1st bound for Menominee, Michigan. When about fifteen miles out of the Sturgeon Bay Ship canal they sighted a burning vessel. After they hove to and checked down on her windward side they found it to be the Str. John Emory Owen. The U. S. Government Lighthouse Tender Sumac, and the Steamer George Burnham had already picked off her crew when the fire first started, leaving the Owen abandoned by all hands and the cook.

J. Emory Owen

She was loaded with a cargo of corn, and most of the fire was at her after end. The A. A. No. 1, after putting out all signs of the fire with her many fire hoses, sent some men over the side to board her and make a tow line fast forward. After they got underway these men steered her by hand as she was towed through the Sturgeon Bay canal and tied her up to the dock on the north side at the west end of the canal. She soon sank and settled on the bottom because the water in her holds from the fire hose in excess to the cargo was too much weight for her to float.

The water here was about 18 feet deep. This left her forward and after cabins dry with very little of her main deck awash, while she rested on the bottom.

About a week later representative of the owners came to claim her and after many months of law suits, the crew during the following winter received $25 apiece for their trouble.

Looking north across Betsie Bay about 1905. The U. S. training ship Yantic fueling at the railroad coal dock above the carferry slips in Elberta. This fuel was all pushed aborad in wheelbarrows. Up the plank and dumped into a hole. Near her bow can be seen one of the many small passenger ferry boats that made good money up, down and across Betsie Bay at 5 cents per trip. Often these training ships would race their boat crews with the crew of the local Coast Guard. The Royal Frontenac Hotel is on the left and the mineral spring bath houses.

During September of 1904, the A. A. No. 1 while making Frankfort Harbor in a big seaway, loosened the quadrant on her rudder stock. This made her helm useless. After tying up in Frankfort they tipped the A. A. No.1 up by running some loaded cars forward and pumping her dry aft. This enabled the crew to get under her stern and unship her rudder. Not having the facilities for repair in Frankfort, Captain Larson and her crew took the A. A. No. 1 to the ship yards in Milwaukee without a rudder--a distance of 142 miles. They steered her with the engines, which was very dangerous and tiresome navigating and would not be allowed today.

In 1904 with Capt. Tulledge still her Master and Fred Brown her Chief Engineer the A. A. No. 1 left Frankfort on February 1st bound for Manitowoc, Wisconsin. When she made the west shore she found the rest of the fleet stuck fast in the ice. After several attempts to break them loose, she got caught in a large windrow of ice and stayed there with the others for 29 days. This was just north of Twin River Point and off the town of Nero.

On January 2, 1905, the A. A. No. 1 left Manitowoc at 5:30 a.m. bound for Frankfort. The wind was N.N.W. strong with a big sea in the lake. They steered up the west shore to get to the northward, high enough to get a good run out of it on the way home with the sea behind her. They had on about half a cargo, eleven cars that made rather a light draft for good performance in a big seaway. Otto Grim was on watch as 2nd Mate and he squared away before the sea too soon. When they picked up the east shore they were way to the southward of Frankfort heading on Burnham Bluff. It was 30 below zero and the wind had increased to gale force with light snow. The sea by this time was so big that each time they would try to swing her up into the sea and wind, trying to get high enough to the windward to make the place, the bit seas would hit her bows with such force

41

she would loose most of her headway and blow around into the trough of the seas against her rudder.

After trying three times and realizing that she was drifting closer and closer to the beach Capt. Larson decided to let her off before the sea. Steering as close to the wind as possible, the A. A. No. 1 finally made Sheboygan, Wisconsin. They laid there for three full days wind bound before starting back home.

The A. A. No. 2, the Ann Arbor office and two grain elevators are on the left the Steamer Northland is just coming in to the hotel dock. She and her sister ship the Northwest both traded here during the resort season.

Steamer Petosky about 1905 outbound from Frankfort and tug Alice Campbell awaiting an inbound tow. She traded out of Frankfort for many years and was at times leased by the railroad on the package freight haul. Ended her days in Sturgeon Bay boneyard December 2, 1935

The Ann Arbor Number 4 was built by the Globe Iron Works at Cleveland, Ohio, November 1906. 259 feet long, 52 ft. beam and of 1884 gross tons.

After all hands had eaten their Thanksgiving dinner they left go the lines and departed Cleveland piers at 1:30 p.m. November 28, 1906, bound for her home port of Frankfort, Michigan, on her maiden voyage.

She encountered heavy weather on her way up, being forced to anchor at Mackinaw for about three days during a northwest snow storm. She arrived home at 10:00 a.m. Friday, December 7, 1906.

After taking aboard fuel, supplies and her first cargo she departed for Manitowoc December 13, 1906. The apron, rails, etc., were a perfect fit at all docks.

The A. A. No. 4 on one of her early trips into the Frankfort Harbor in the spring of 1907.

During the latter part of September in 1906, the A. A. No. 3 was enroute from Manistique to Frankfort and when abreast of the South Fox Isle a two masted schooner hove into sight almost dead ahead. Coming closer they could see that she had distress signals flying (the American flag floated upside down) and that she was named the Senator. The A. A. No. 3 drifted down alongside her and sent down some men on a Jacob's ladder. They found her abandoned, loaded with coal and about half full of water. They got a fire going in her donkey boiler, started the pump, took aboard a tow line from the A. A. No. 3 and towed into Frankfort, Here they made her well fast to the dock by the Ann Arbor Office and left two men aboard to keep her dry. One night after they had banked the fire and gone ashore, a crew came over her side and sailed her out to sea. Later the owners sent the Captain and chief of the A. A. No. 3 each $12.00, the Engineers and Mates, $7.50, and each of the crew $2.00 apiece.

The A. A. No.s 1 and 2 in foreground and the No.s 3 and 4 near the slip. Windbound about 1906. The Royal Frontenac Hotel can be seen in the background. This picture clearly shows how much farther forward the deck had been cut on the A. A. No. 2.

On February 25, 1907, at 4:00 a.m. with the wind easterly, light and cloudy, the A. A. No. 2 left Manistique with a full cargo bound for Frankfort. After she was about four hours on her way the wind shifted to the N.W. and blew a regular gale with snow.

They arrived outside Frankfort about noon and keeping her well to the windward of the place they opened her engines up for all the speed she had and took a run at the harbor entrance, running before the sea. Just as her nose was outside of the piers and when nearing the shallow water at the entrance (or smelling the bottom) a monstrous sea came roaring along, striking the A. A. No. 2 broadside to port, which caused her to yaw around against her hard over rudder, driving her bow down onto the outer end of the south pier. She fetched up standing with a terrific jar that knocked most everyone off his feet, bounding back out to sea and taking almost the entire outside crib from the outer end of the south pier with her.

This sudden jar caused a large oak block to break through the car deck grating and fall into the cross head slide of the horizontal port engine, causing it to jam and stop working. The Captain headed her south before the sea, and let her go where she steered the best, combing the beach.

Running before the wind with only one engine working she did not have speed enough to keep away from the big seas that climbed up and rolled in upon her open stern.

She shipped aboard more water than her pumps could carry away, and the A. A. No. 2 slowly started to submerge. Most of the crew realizing that their only hope to day afloat was in getting the jammed engine free again, made a run for the engine room to assist the Chief and Old Sam. This wooden block was jammed so solidly that it had to be chipped out in small pieces, which was very slow work. By this time the sea water in the engine room and firehold was knee deep and very cold. Some of the wooden gratings covering the manholes on the engine room floor had floated away and now and then one of the boys would step into these open holes and almost disappear into the bilge, having to be fished out by others.

Finally they released the block, but the steam having dropped down from 120 pounds to 40 pounds would hardly turn both engines over and keep the pump going. The water in the fire hold was almost up to the fire boxes. Old Sam and his gang had to pass down dry coal from the top of the piles and nurse the steam back up while standing waist deep in ice water.

As the steam pressure crawled back up, the A. A. No. 2 gained more headway, creeping away from the seas and keeping her decks dry. The pump also started working faster and slowly lowered the imprisoned water in her hull. By this time they were just North of Onekama and realizing that she would never come around into the sea for another try at Frankfort they decided to take a chance on Onekama Harbor.

Although the A. A. No. 2 was away deep aft being so full of water, they felt certain that with a little luck she could make the place, having seen the Steamer Oscar T. Flint trading there drawing 18 feet of water. So with everything placed in the best possible condition under the circumstances they headed for the harbor with a prayer and made it.

They tied up at the lumber dock and started the pump going wide open at 4 p.m. on the 25th and pumped all night until about 1 p.m. on the 26th. They left Onekama at 2 p.m. and arrived and tied up in Frankfort at 4:30 p.m.

The A. A. No. 2, after laying in Frankfort for three days making minor repairs, went to the dry dock in Milwaukee ship yards. She was ready for sea again in about a week.

The A. A. No. 2 being assisted through heavy ice by the tug Annie L. Smith. Winter 1907.

The A. A. No. 3 left Frankfort at 7:20 p.m. on October 8th with the No. 1 in tow. After being outside about one hour the wind went N.W. blowing a regular "gagger". Realizing that it would be useless to try to buck this gale back to Frankfort with the No. 1 in tow, Capt. Larson aboard the No. 3 decided to square off before the wind and make a run for Onekema. He was in hopes of arriving there before the sea started to make. The No. 3 running wide open made the harbor O.K. but when the No. 1 neared the shallow water she took a sheer to the left and piled up on the sandy beach just north of the piers, with the piers between her and the No. 3 and the tow line racking everything off the top of the sea wall.

The wind stayed N.W. and blew hard during the next four days, while the No. 1 with the motion of the sea settled deeper and deeper on the sandy beach. On October 13th the wind moderated and the No. 4 came down from Frankfort to assist the No.s 1 and 3. After the No.s 3 and 4 had made their tow lines fast to the No. 1. They pulled all that day and night in an effort to drag the No. 1 out into deep water. Although they jerked on their lines(parting them often) and pulled at various angles the No. 1 refused to budge. On the morning of the 14th, the No. 4 dropped her anchor outside and backed down, first on one side of the No. 1 and then on the other. Using her wheels as a dredge, washing the sand out from under the No. 1 and slowly but surely making a dredge channel from the beached vessel out to sea. Late that night the No. 4 in making her stern fast to the No. 1 parted a manila line and as the loose end fell under her stern the current from her wheels sucked the line around the shaft of her starboard propeller. As the wheel kept turning it wrapped the line tighter and tighter and acting as a compressor it stopped this engine.

The No. 4 then let go her lines, hove up the hook and made Frankfort with only her port engine operating. Here she tipped her stern up and cleared the disabled wheel by cutting the line off.

When the A. A. No. 4 left the scene, the No. 3 came in from outside, worked down to the No. 1, made her tow line well fast and after six hours of steady pulling and with the aid of a strong offshore wind, dragged the No. 1 off the beach and into the channel that the No. 4 had made and out into deep water. They then headed back to Frankfort, arriving there at 12:50 p.m. on October 15th. After refueling, taking aboard some new tow lines, etc., They left Frankfort bound for Milwaukee the second time at 6:15 a.m. October 16th. Expecting more westerly weather, they steered for the lee of the west shore, making the land at Twin River Point just north of Manitowoc, thence down the beach to Milwaukee, Wisconsin. The No. 1 was in the yards there for 64 days and received a general overhauling.

In 1908 the A. A. No. 1 was sent out from Frankfort to go on the Northport to Manistique and often when the freight here was heavy, the A. A. No. 2 came up to assist her. Here they replaced the carferry Manistique then owned by the Manistique and Northern R. R. The carferry Manistique was then in the ship yards at South Chicago for two months, being repaired after striking the rocky bottom at the east side of entrance to Manistique Harbor. The carferry Manistique was sold late in 1908 to the Grand Trunk R.R.. for $1,000,000 and renamed the Milwaukee. She foundered off Racine while battling one of the biggest northerly seas that ever rolled down that 250-mile stretch of open water between Manistique, Michigan and Wind Point, Wisconsin, on October 22, 1929, with the loss of 51 sailors and the cook. She was enroute from Milwaukee to Grand Haven with a full cargo aboard. She is listed with many others as a ship that never returned. Few know where she went, how, or why. Perhaps the fact that freight cars increased in length, etc., from 30 feet long for which she was original built to carry in 1903 to 50 feet in length when she was lost in '29 may have had something to do with this disaster, as in the case of the sinking of the A. A. No. 4 in 1923.

Ann Arbor No. 2 entering the harbor. This shows here decks and sides cut away. One of her last trips before she was tied up at the old ice house.

Old ferry dock in foreground. The passenger ferry Pottawattomie is at the dock and the Steamer Petosky is leaving the old Northern Michigan Transit Co. dock. The A. A. No.s 1 and 2 in and near the slip across the bay. (About 1908).

January 24, 1909 at 5:00 a.m. wind easterly, fresh and snow, she went on the rocky shore at Pt. Aux Barques enroute to Manistique, Michigan.

Captain Robertson then Master, sent Charles Robertson and Lester Cooper ashore in a long boat to phone assistance from a tug at Manistique. After parking their boat they headed down the ice covered beach for the town of Thompson, some eight miles away.

Here they placed the call and after a few refreshments, started back, finally arriving at their small boat, but when looking seaward, they discovered the A. A. No. 4 gone. During their absence the wind had shifted to the southward causing her to release herself, riding the swell it then made.

Hungry, footsore and leg weary they built a large fire and spent the night in the hull of an old schooner that had come ashore some years ago. They caught the A. A. No. 4 at Manistique on her next trip.

May 29, 1909. the A. A. No. 4 rolled over in the slip at Manistique. This was caused by too much weight placed on one side while loading a heavy cargo of iron ore. As she slowly listed over on her side, the water coming in the neglected open portholes, between decks, was discovered much too late. The crew had sufficient time to gather some of their belongings and disembark. Tug Favorite in command of Capt. Cunningham with the assistance of the wrecking crew righted her on June 25, 1909. Towing her to Frankfort the next day.

The A. A. No. 4 on side in slip at Manistique.

The A. A. No. 4 with the tug Favorite alongside. The A. A. No. 2 on right at city dock, The A. A. No. 3 with split cabin in the background. Although the regular slip and apron were out of commission at this time they built a portable apron and shipped cargoes on a regular schedule.

Divers at work on wreck of the A. A. No. 4.

The A. A. No. 4 after she was righted and towed to Frankfort. The damage to her side can be seen.

She arrived at Manitowoc shipyards July 15, was at sea again September 27, 1909.

Early in March of 1910 after having been stuck fast for a week in a heavy ice flow enroute from Manistique to Frankfort, the A. A. No. 1 was sent to Manitowoc, Wisconsin. While she was tied up there in the North Western slip fully loaded with 20 freight cars aboard, containing lumber, charcoal, merchandise, etc., she caught fire. The cause of which is unknown to this day.

The fire started at 4:30 p.m. March 8, 1910, and at noon of the next day she burned to her water edge. Two of her crew members that were asleep forward awoke to late to scamper aft and off her stern, so they had to jump over the bow and swim ashore.

The A. A. No. 1 was all rebuilt about one year before and was then in ship shape condition. She and her cargo were covered by insurance and the total loss was about $1,000,000.

The Love Construction Co. out of Muskegon, Michigan, bought her hull, towed it across the lake and used it as a sand scow.

Ann Arbor No. 1 burning at the C.&N.W. slip in Manitowoc in 1910. the A. A. No. 3 is standing by across her bow. Smoke can be seen coming out of the portholes which had recently replaced the windows.

Remains of the A. A. No. 1 after her burning.

Launching of the Ann Arbor No. 5 in 1910.

The Ann Arbor No. 5 was launched at the Toledo shipyard in the fall of 1910. The A. A. No. 5 was built as an icebreaker, for heavy winter ice had often held up the other boats in the fleet. Often forced to break ice more than 2 feet thick, she was known to have made her way through more than 36 inches of solid blue ice, and in 20 feet of water to have pushed through fields of ice that extended to the bottom. Not only did she lead the way, making channels for the other ships of the line to follow, but she was also the fastest ship, making records on all the runs from the Frankfort-Elberta harbor to the cross lake ports of Manitowoc and Kewaunee, Wisconsin and Menominee and Manistique, Michigan.

The A. A. No. 5 arrived at her home port of Frankfort on January 11, 1911, and a great celebration was held, with people coming from miles around to get a look at the new ship.

The A. A. No. 5's first trip into Frankfort, flags flying.

The A. A. No. 5 came out with very narrow and lofty smokestacks which were nicknamed "Saw-mill" stacks. They were out of proportion to the rest of her construction and gave her an odd appearance, particularly when under way with a clear sky as a background.

After the A. A. No. 5 came out in 1910 the A. A. No. 2 was only placed in service during periods of excess freight. The last time she ever carried a cargo was on September 29, 1912.

During the big fire of the Frontenac Hotel in Frankfort in 1912, the A. A. No. 2 caught fire three different times from the sparks, although she was moored about one mile away.

Mr. Tousley was General Manager of the Ann Arbor Railroad in 1914, and he sold the A. A. No. 2 for $2,000 to Mr. Tom Ray of the Manistee Iron Works. The A. A. No. 4 towed her out of Frankfort to Manistee on October 10, 1914. Here they cut her down and sold most of her for scrap. One of her boilers went in the lumber hooker Marshall F. Butters and the other in the Steamer Petoskey. The Manistee Iron Works sold her hull to the Nicholson Transit Company of Detroit on February 29, 1916. She left Manistee on May 16, 1916, for Detroit. For many years she was used in the St. Claire and Detroit River for a sand sucker called The Whale. Thus ended the lives of the first two carferries on the great lakes.

Fire drill on the A. A. No. 4, 1910

On several other occasions these wooden ships struck breakwaters and rocky bottoms, but other than the jar disturbing the sleep of their crew's and making the Masters and Chief Engineers swear once in a while, they seldom did much damage.

During bad weather they were very good sea boats and had a nice easy roll. They always creaked and groaned while diving into a sea, which often caused the check whistles to blow. This sound had very little rhythm and was most disturbing.

When the watches below were called they always moved their heads with great care, as often one's hair would be caught fast in the cracks of the bulkhead (wall) which opened and closed while rolling. They also had cracks in their wooden hulls below the waterline that would open during her rise and fall while climbing over a big sea. These cracks would of course let sea water seep in. So it was always customary for the engine room crew to keep a supply of old overalls, etc. on hand, cut into strips, which they would force into these winking cracks as she rolled and labored in a seaway.

[Copied from the Keewaunee Paper of January 6, 1911, It said that the new boat had been turned over to the R. R. no date] Also that she could carry 30 long cars or 34 mixed cars, that she was 378 ft x 56 ft and 21 ft. deep. 2 triple expansion engines, 4 Scotch boilers and that Tulledge was master, Henry Erbe 1st mate and W. J. Sweeney was Chief Engineer. In the Kewaunee paper of January 20, 1911, it said that she made her first trip in Kewaunee and that she was the largest carferry in the world.

On January 12, 1911, she hit the rocks close to the south breakwater when entering Manistique harbor. This tore off her starboard shaft and wheel.

Capt. O. B. Olson was on the bow at this time. He thinking they were nearing bad water, tightened his rope yarn belt and sung out to the captain that the was to close. Just then she struck and the captain answered, "I know it now!"

On January 28, 1911, at 8:40 p.m. the A. A. No. 3 left Manistique fully loaded bound for Frankfort. The wind was fresh from the southeast with snow. After clearing the harbor the Captain, intending to hold her up enough to make a good run, hauled her to the eastward too soon and she fetched up on the rocks, pounding her bottom as she rode the incoming swell. (Note: this is about the same place where the A. A. No.s 2, 4 and carferry Manistique went on before). They kept her going ahead and she fought her way out to deep water, leaking badly, and but for her water bottom, perhaps would still be there. She stove in several plates almost the entire length of her bottom, but the only place that the water gained on her pump's was in the engine room. They drove wedges, pillows and rags into these cracks and kept her afloat. After about four hours she made the lee of the east shore and proceeded, badly beaten, into Frankfort. After dispatching her cargo she went to the yard in Milwaukee and was there for over a month undergoing repairs.

At 4:50 a.m. on April 10, 1912, the A. A. No. 5 arrived in Manitowoc Harbor with a full cargo of freight from Frankfort for the Chicago & North Western R. R. Slip (Now known as the lake front dock) in Manitowoc, Wisconsin. Having exchanged cargoes at 8:20 a.m. she left the slip and started to return trip home. The wind was S.S.E. strong with light rain. While winding around in the harbor basin, in an effort to get lined up for the wide-open dash at the seemingly narrow harbor entrance and into the ever freedom of the open sea beyond, the A. A. No. 5 fetched up with her stern against the clay bottom on the north side of the channel, bending her rudder, and damaging her port shaft. She then returned to the slip and after unloading her cargo proceeded up the river to the shipyards where she remained out of service for 6 days repairing the shaft and shipping a new rudder

The A. A. No. 4 in Milwaukee dry dock October 14, 1911

October 14, 1911, enroute from Menominee to Manistique, just after passing through the once seen, never forgotten, picturesque Rock Island passage, the A. A. No. 4 fetched up on a 11-ft spot at full speed damaging several plates. The A. A. No. 3 pulled her off. She then went to the Milwaukee shipyards for repairs. Placed back in service again November 10, 1911.

The captain was entirely exonerated of this grounding. He had left a call for 8:30 but the mate and wheelsman, spinning yarns of old, neglected this. Therefore he was awakened from a sound sleep with that ever stomach sickening feeling of a rumbling, groaning stranded keel.

The A. A. No.s 3 with 1 and 2 outside stuck in ice.

February 11, 1912, the A. A. No.s 3, 4 and 5 left Frankfort bound for Manistique, traveling together because of the lake being full of heavy ice. Outside Manistique the A. A. No.s 3 and 4, got stuck fast in a big windrow of ice about 500 ft. wide. The No. 5 after several attempts to break through this windrow, backed out, changed her course, hauled to westward and coming behind it near the town of Thompson. She made good time and after entering Manistique, unloading and loading her cargo, she backed out to assist the No.s 3 and 4 to exchange their cargoes. After this was done, they started back for home with the A. A. No. 5 in the lead at 9:00 a.m. February 15th.

They followed the west shore down, arriving abreast of Pottawattmie light on Rock Island at 5 p.m. on the 17th. Here they stopped for the night, close to, of course, so the crews could all visit. The next morning the A. A. No.s 3 and 4 were frozen fast. the A. A. No. 5 broke them loose.

February 19th broke out all hands and spudded the A. A. No. 4 loose. She in turn broke out the A. A. No.s 3 and 5. This fleet arrived in Frankfort at noon February 20th.

After taking aboard fuel, supplies, etc. the A. A. No. 4 left Frankfort at 6:00 a.m. on the 21st bound for Manitowoc.

At this time Capt. Alexander Larson was Master of the A. A. No. 4. On this trip he and Ole Glarum laid off to attend the wedding of his brother, O.T. Larson.

This left the A. A. No. 4 in charge of the first mate. Wind was northeast, fresh with snow. After making the west shore, while looking for the harbor, she fetched up on the beach. This was about one mile north of Manitowoc. She pounded her bottom heavily, riding the swell. She seemed to be on a big rock. They put the wheel hard over and she came back out in the lake by herself, badly beaten. After getting outside of this sound pocket they picked up the foghorn and got inside.

Although her cargo was for the Soo line, they backed into the NW slip to unload, as it was much nearer. The incoming water gained on her pumps, sinking the A. A. No. 4 lower and lower.

When arriving at the slip, her stern was way below the apron. To overcome this they had to fill in with timbers, blocks, etc. This caused a steep grade and it took all the power in two locomotives coupled together, to unload her. After unloading they worked a large canvas jacket over the hole and pumped her out. In spite of the ice passed enroute she made it to the Milwaukee shipyard. She was back in service again April 15, 1912.

At this time our well remembered shipmate, one of the best sailors ever to be brought up under the canvas, Captain Samuel Nelson was 1st mate here. Being on the bow, he hailed the bridge, saying "We are to far to the northward." But the captain, being a little stubborn, on hearing this, ordered the quartermaster to port a point. This brought her wider on the place, taking to the beach.

A. W. Lucky in Benton Harbor

Early in the spring of 1912 (April) the Schooner A. W. Lucky and the A. A. No. 3 met in dense fog near Sherwood Point in Green Bay. The wooden schooner sheered off the steel boy and slid by with the loss of her headgear, boom and bowsprit. After ascertaining the damage she was towed to Menominee for repair.

On May 21, 1913, Wind S.W. strong with heavy fog, the A. A. No. 5 eastbound slipping out of a dense fog bank just outside Frankfort saw the Steamer Missouri dead ahead making a try for the harbor. The A. A. No. 5 immediately checked down to allow the Steamer Missouri ample time to arrive inside and tie up, thus leaving the harbor clear for the docking of the No. 5. While watching the Steamer Missouri approach the piers, through his binoculars, Captain Tulledge was surprised to see her fetch up with the bluff off her starboard bow against the south pier and after being carried safely inside by the following seas, she bumped herself along the north pier and into the inner harbor where she tied up. (Later it became known that she had done herself very

63

little damage.) In those days the piers were made of wood and as they had some give to them ships often bounced off with little or no damage. Quite different from the solid cement ones of today.

Having trouble with the steering gear sticking and not being able to swing the rudder all the way over, after striking the bottom while eastbound through the Sturgeon Bay Canal on September 22, they decided to go the ship yards in Milwaukee for repairs. After exchanging cargo's in Frankfort they took on a full load for Manitowoc, unloading there they headed South down the west shore for Milwaukee. Here they were assisted into the drydock by the Tugs W.H. Simpsen and J. J. Hagerman. While there they repaired the steering engine, shipped a new rudder and after making other minor repairs put to sea again on October 1. In a very short time here steering engine started bucking again and some of the old timers still in action today loved to wink their weather eye and tell how the A. A. No. 5, while the engineers were trying to make adjustments on the steering engine made several trips across the lake without the use of her rudder. This was done by steering her with the main engines. After her engineers had given up all hopes of repairing the steering machinery the No. 4 took the No. 5 in tow on Oct. 21st and started for the shipyards in Milwaukee. On arrival there she was met by an expert from Toledo Shipbuilding Co. of Toledo Ohio, where the engine was built. After he had some changes made in the steering engine, the No. 5 was again placed in operation and since then has had but few repairs made in her steering apparatus.

On December 9, 1912, the A. A. No. 5 departed Manitowoc breakwater at 5:15 a.m. with a full load for Frankfort. The wind was S.S.W. strong and clear. She steered the regular course N.E. by E. until the wind increased to gale force at 7:30 a.m. with snow flurries. Not wanting to be caught on the weather shore in a big sea with poor visibility Capt. Tulledge slanted her back for the lee of the west shore steering where she rode the best and gradually, as she lost the sea worked her up high enough to make or find shelter in Sturgeon Bay Canal. Arriving there at 1 p.m. they turned around just east of the bridge and tied up in the canal to await weather. During the night the wind moderated some and shifted more to the westward, so at 6:00 a.m. on the 10th, the A. A. No. 5 left the canal and headed for home. As the east shore hove into sight between snow squalls the Captain decided that the sea was to big to make the place so he changed the course and headed for the shelter of the South Manitou Isle Harbor. Arriving here in the lee of the high sandy bluffs at 11:30 a.m. she checked down and gently slid her sharp bow up onto the sandy beach, and slowly worked one engine ahead to keep her there. They awaited weather until the following day December 11th when the wind moderated and shifted to the N.W. Then at 9:00 a.m. she backed off the beach and again headed for home and arrived there at 2:00 p.m.

Running before a big westerly sea on February 5th the A. A. No. 5 nearing Frankfort at 9:00 a.m. sighted the rest of the fleet the No.s 3 & 4 stuck fast in the slush ice just outside the harbor entrance. Capt. Robertson then rang up the No. 5 for everything she had and took a wide-open run for the narrow space left between the two imprisoned ships in hopes that he could break a channel near them, through which the No.s 3 and 4 could follow the No. 5 into the harbor. But the ice was much heavier than expected and the No. 5 slowly lost her way and gradually came to a sliding stop just inside the rolling surge of the big sea outside. The No. 5 was not stuck but the Captain decided it was best to let her lay until a shift of wind came. This would release the pressure on the ice making it possible to get underway with enough headway to break the other boats loose and proceed on into the harbor. After laying there all day the 6th, 7th and 8th within a mile from home, the wind finally on February 9th died out and worked to the northward releasing the pressure at noon that day the No. 5 had broken out Boats 3 and 4 and escorted them inside the harbor.

Because of the burning of the No. 1 and the inspection laws condemning the old No. 2 the Ann Arbor fleet was cut down to a three-boat operation, thus whenever freight became to heavy the A. A. leased a boat from the P. M. During the year of 1913 and up until the A. A. No. 6 came out in 1917 several of their ships traded in here also the carferry Maitland No. 1.

The Maitland No. 1

February 10th 1913, the A. A. No. 5 departed Frankfort at 12:20 p.m. bound for Keewaunee. Steering the regular course of WxS¼S with wind S. S. E fresh and cloudy. When about 2 hours out the wind shifted to due south with gale force and snow. the A. A. No. 5 then had to hold up into the wind and sea to stop from rolling and get high enough to the windward to make the place. At 7:00 p.m. they were south of Twin River Point and decide to square away for Keewaunee. After calling the engine room for everything she had they let her come around on a hard right wheel. While coming around, she got caught in the trough between two big seas which slowed up her swing and while she was rolling deeply and fighting to get the sea behind her she tipped over a ton of coal from the starboard wing into the side of a wooden box car in the same center. Spilling the coal and smashing in the entire side of the box car, making real mess which took the section gang 8 hours to clean up after their arrival in

Kewaunee at 10:00 p.m. that night. In the old days the tipping over of cars and other damage of freight caused by heavy rolling was quite common but today all carferries are equipped with most modern navigational instruments this is seldom, if ever heard of.

On March 10th the A. A. No. 5 while maneuvering around the Keewaunee harbor trying to make the skip, with a strong N. wind blowing drifted down onto the fish tug Maude S. of Marinette, Wisconsin, and carried away some of her upper works. Two months later to the day May 10th. The No. 5 again entered Keewaunee harbor and conditions were the same wind N. and the fish tug Maude S. laying tied up in the same place (only turned around) so the Captain smiling being not in the mood to help rebuild a new boat of her other side stopped the A. A. No. 5 and let her lay while he sent the boys ashore to move the fish tug until the A. A. No. 5 was made fast in the slip. The owner of the Maude S then decided that the Captain did not want to buy her for the insurance so he found a new parking place for her.

March 16th, the A. A. No. 5 departed Manistique at 1:30 a.m. with a full load bound for Frankfort, steering due south the wind was N.E. Fresh and snow. At 6:30 a. m. when abreast of the Manitous they sighted the lights of the A. A. No. 4 on the left bow. Coming closer they heard her blowing four long blasts of her whistle (Signal for help or tug at sea) the A. A. No. 5 then altered her course, checked her speed and came to a dead stop in the heavy ice along side of the No. 4. The No. 4 was north bound for Manistique and had orders from the Frankfort office for the A. A. No. 5 to stop at both islands and pickup some passengers for Frankfort. The A. A. No. 4 then continued on her way and the A. A. No. 5 broke her way through the ice and into the dock at the N. Manitou Island arriving there at 9:00 a.m. after taking aborad several Islanders she departed at 10:00 a. m. and headed for the old dock in the almost land backed bay of the S. Manitou Isle, here she took aboard some more passengers and departed for Frankfort at noon the same day.

Years ago when the ice became heavy in Green Bay

navigation closed there for the winter and freight for Menominee was routed down to Manitowoc or around the lake. The first boat then to pass through the canal and Sturgeon bay was a most welcome sight and a sure sign of spring. People crowded the bay shores waving their arms and hats the steamer in return blew continuous salutes with the big whistle. The A. A. No. 5 was the first boat to open navigation in the spring of 1913 on April 9th.

April 24th the A. A. No. 5 departed Frankfort bound for Manitowoc at 3:30 p.m. course S.W.xW. and the wind was S. fresh and fog. After running her regular time of 5 hours to abreast of the point at Two Rivers and not hearing any fog whistle the Captain thinking that she was wide on the place hauled her in a point making her course W.S.W. Not being sure of her running time, they checked 20 minutes later to give her a cast with the hand lead to find out the water depth under her. Shortly after the engineers received the check , the A. A. No. 5 fetched up standing on the sandy bottom between Two Rivers and the point. With the stillness that came when she stopped operations they could hear the fog horn both at Two Rivers and the point. After the watch had checked over her bottom for any sign of a leak the Captain proceeded to back her off, at first he tried to jump her loose by working her from full ahead to full astern. As the did not budge her he started to swing her from hard over wheel to the other with this she gave a slight respond and in a short time she was swinging several points of the compass and during one of these good swings he again backed her wide open and she let go the bottom forward and slide back on an even fore and aft keel into the deeper water and was soon under way after being on the beach for 30 minutes with no apparent damage.

September 6th, the A. A. No. 5 left Frankfort breakwater at 9:15 a.m. steering the regular course of WxS ¼ S for Kewaunee. The wind was S. S. E. fresh with light fog. At 1:50 a.m. the next morning October 7th the lookout on the bow sung out that he could hear the fog horn. Ten minutes later they lost the sound of the horn and checked down to slow speed. At 2:05

Boat 5 fetched up with a lifting grinding jar on the rocky beach 3/4 of a mile south of the piers. After backing at full speed for several minutes, the Captain gave the orders to fill her up aft with water and move the freight cars on the car deck aft as far as possible in order to tip her by the stern. After this was done he backed her again and at 6 a.m. she came away clear of the beach. By this time the wind had shifted to the westward and cleared the fog. She arrived in the slip in Keewaunee at 6:30 a.m. and much to the surprise of all hands they could find no leaks nor bottom damage.

The A. A. No. 5 while coming out of the slip in Kewaunee with the wind abeam found it necessary to give her the gun and get some headway on her in order to keep her from drifting down onto the Schooner Marsh that was tied up on the city side of the channel. In passing her with this speed the A. A. No. 5 parted the mooring lines on the schooner and set her adrift. Later the Company received a nice fat repair bill to cover this. (During their time the carferries have paid many a repair bill on old packets that otherwise would of sank before their time.)

December 2, 1913, the A. A. No. 5 departed Frankfort for Manistique. Wind N.E. Fresh with snow and the course N ½ E. When just north of Point Betsie they heard a steamer blowing four long whistles a short distance to the windward. The A. A. No. 5 then altered her course and bore down on the vessel soon she was seen through the falling snow. Coming nearer the A. A. No. 5 checked down and as the sea was flat came to a dead stop within speaking distance of the lee side. She proved to be the Steamer Quincy A. Shaw south bound for Chicago with a load of coal and on her last trip of the season. She had come through Mackinaw with clear weather and after leaving Lansing Shoal started down the west shore, but when the wind shifted to the eastward with snow the Captain being late decided to pull over and follow the lee shore. After running out his time and having just an old oil compass that perhaps was not to true on eastwardly headings and sill no bottom on the hand lead. He decided that he was lost at sea and thinking that he was close to Point Betsie he started blowing the four distress whistles to attract their attention. The A. A. No. 5 then let her line up alongside to compared compass headings and assisted them in setting a soft course down the east shore then with a parting salute, disappeared in the heavy snow and back on her course.

January 11, 1914, the A. A. No. 5 while running before a big north west sea trying to make the harbor at Frankfort was caught between two large seas that carried her down onto the outer of the south pier. The jar of this stove in several plates on her starboard bow. After unloading her cargo she departed for the ship yards in Milwaukee and while there repairing the bow she was placed in the dry dock for the hull inspection and had new sleeves put in both tail shafts. She was at sea again on January 26th. On February 10th she tied up at the sheer legs at Manitowoc for 3 days and shipped two new smoke stacks.

September 21, 1914, the A. A. No. 5 was delayed for 6 hours in Frankfort while loading on supplies and material to be used while in Manistee for repairs at the Manistee Iron Works. The A. A. No. 5 left Frankfort at 5:05 a.m. wind S fresh and clear, course S ½ W. Arrived Manistee Breakwater at 7:30 a.m. and without the use of a tug tied up at the Iron Works at 9:15 a.m. While there they scraped and painted the hull and inside the cabins made several repairs to machinery also rebored and bushed the air pumps and replaced new fuming posts on the car deck. Late in the afternoon of October 11th the A. A. No. 5 was ready for sea once more but the captain decided to await daylight the next morning before starting down the river and into the lake. The A. A. No. 5 departed Manistee at 7:00 a.m. October 12 bound for the home port of Frankfort to pick up a cargo and return into service again. The late Rom Ray founder of the Iron Works was often complimented on the nice work and efficiency of his shops. The A. A. No. 5 being the largest boat ever to come there for repairs.

December 18, 1914 the A. A. No. 5 departed Keewaunee

breakwater at 5:25 a.m. bound for Frankfort wind S.W. fresh and cloudy. Working up to windward steering due S.E. for one hour 25 minutes and then as she would have the sea well behind her they squared off for home steering N.E.xE½E. At 8:30 a.m. the wind increased to gale force with snow so they headed back for the lee of the west shore and arrived outside Keewaunee at noon and having lost the sea checked down and let her drift. The wind became fluffy at 3 p.m. so they worked her back to the south ward and when just off the point at Two Rivers they again headed for home steering NE by E at 5 p.m. But at 9:00 p.m. the wind breezed up and as it was snowing harder than ever they again headed back for the shelter of the west shore where they hung off under check until the wind started to work more to the northward. Then at 3:00 a.m. the next day they set the course for home and made it. Arriving there at 7:15 a. m. after spending 25 hours 50 minutes on the lake.

December 13th, the A. A. No. 5 with a heavy load left the slip in Frankfort at 4:05 a.m. with everything on her wide open. Making a run at the big N.W. sea roll in the piers. As her bow rose to meet the wind driven sea outside her squaring stern struck bottom just at the pier entrance and broke a blade off her port propeller. This uneven balance of her wheel caused a vibration and they found it necessary to run the engine under check, which slowed her speed. On her return trip to Frankfort she was delayed 19 hours while they tipped up and shipped a new bucket.

January 6, 1916, the A. A. No. 5 departed Frankfort at 9:15 a.m. bound for Menominee Michigan steering WxN, wind W gale, steam and snow. Arrived the Sturgeon Bay Canal at 2:05 p.m. when abreast of Sherwood Point at 3:15 p.m. she struck a heavy windrow of ice anchored to the bottom and became stuck fast. After tipping her down by the stern by filling her compartments aft with water and running the cars on the car deck back, they were able to back her off. At 11:00 p.m. after the Captain made a few more tries at the heavy ice here, he decided to turn around and proceed to Menominee by the way of Death

Door Passage. They came out through the canal east bound at 1:00 a.m. on January 7th. Steered N. E. for 45 minutes then N. x E. ½ E. wind in lake was N. W. light and clear. Cana Isle bore abreast at 2:55 a.m. Hauled in on the red ranges on Plum Isle at 3:30 a.m. N.W. N. ¼ N Pilot Isle 3:55 a.m. Plum Isle 405 a.m. W.N.W. hauled 4:15 a.m. W ¼ N Door Bluff at 4:30 a.m. course W x S ½ S. Chambers Isle 5:45 a.m. S.W ½ W Arrived at the piers at Menominee at 7:00 a.m. also took the door passage back home. Although she lost some time in the ice crossing the bay she did much better this long way around as she was not stuck once.

February 21, 1916, the A. A. No. 5 arrived at the breakwater at Manitowoc, Wisconsin, and after poking her nose inside the harbor she found the ice very heavy decided to turn around and back up the river to the Soo Line Slip. While working her way up the river stern first she fell wind abeam down against the Steam Barge S.J. Crouse and did some damage to her hull. In Manitowoc Harbor, as there is not to much room in the river near the Soo Line slip for turning around the carferries, during the ice months often turn in the spacious harbor entrance and back up the river. This often saves a lot of time.

After spending a week in the ship yard in Manitowoc for general repairs, replacing three broken buckets on the starboard propeller that were slightly damaged in the heavy winter ice in Green Bay, the A. A. No. 5 was at sea again on June 20th. Leaving Manitowoc she proceeded to Frankfort and loaded for Manistique. Arriving there at noon on June 21st, and while maneuvering around in the harbor making a landing she had the misfortune of striking the rocky bottom and broke off the same three buckets on her starboard wheel. Exchanging cargos she left for Frankfort and after unloading there she was delayed for 30 hours while tipping up and one again replacing the sea buckets.

September 26, 1916 we have the first mention of a carferry being delayed while loading autos. This was while loading at Menominee.

November 23, 1916 the A. A. No. 5 departed Frankfort at 12:55 a.m. steering S.W.xW¼ W for Manitowoc. Wind S. E. light and foggy with rain squalls. Not having heard nor seen a thing at 6:25 a.m. they checked down to listen and take a sounding with the hand lead. As she lost her way the watch on the forsil deck heard the fog horn well on the left bow. The Master thinking that they were in to close and to the north wharf of the place ordered the wheel hard a starboard (today hard left) and rang full speed ahead on the starboard engine to help her swing away from the land. While swinging on a hard over wheel she fetched up aft on her starboard quarter with a terrible thumping noise that caused her to roll as she fought her self clear of the rocky bottom. Immediate examination showed, no leaks, rudder would not respond to a hard over wheel and that the starboard engine raced as though there was but little wheel or propeller left. Still able to hear the fog horn the captain headed her in on it. Being in the crippled condition, the Captain when near the harbor blew four long the whistle is for the assistance of a tug that met them just inside and helped them into the slip. Arriving there at 9:00 a.m. they unloaded and tied up at the Cheese dock awaiting orders. At 2:00 a.m. they started water running into the forward holds to tip her up enough to check her rudder and propellers. This they did and found a bent rudder and the starboard wheel missing, the shaft had been broken off at the bracket. They also found 7 badly corrugated plates that later had to be taken off rerolled in the yard. She laid at the cheese dock for 4 more days waiting for room in dry dock. and on November 28th the tug towed her outside to dump ashes and refill her all drinking water tanks. Returning inside they proceeded up the river and into the dry dock. Arriving the at 3:00 p.m. on December 11th she was again in service.

In 1916 there was an excess of freight on all railroads due to the first World War. To overcome this the Ann Arbor Railroad leased the carferry Maitland No. 1, which operated out of Frankfort for about four months that year.

The railroad also purchased her sister ship that was then

being built at Detroit and renamed her the Steamer Ann Arbor No. 6. She is 350 feet long, with 56 foot beam, makes 14 miles per hour, and besides passengers carries an average load of 26 freight cars.

City of Charlevoix. Backing away from the old North Michigan dock at Frankfort with freight and passengers on her run from Chicago to Mackinac. She had a rugged life, coming out as the Champlain and burned with the loss of several lives near Charlevoix. Raised and rebuilt as in the picture. Later renamed Kansas and ended her career burning in Manistee. Notice Ann Arbor No. 3 with old split cabin, elevator and life saving station across the bay, about 1916. She burned in Manistee October 27, 1924.

United States Life Saving Service at Frankfort harbor. Surf boat drill. In the early days these gallant men in their small boats put to sea in foul and fair weather and rowed many milese to aid a ship and crew in distress, etc. Often they would venture outside when tugs and larger craft refused to brave the weather. On various holidays they would put on a spectacular drill while the water front was lined with townsfolk and visitors.

The winter of 1916-17 was considered by marine men to be the worst winter for ice since 1904. Due to this condition it was thought the ship would not be able to get out of the St. Clair river until spring unless the company was willing to spend extra money to get her through earlier.

As the railroad was so badly in need of another boat they decided to get her to Frankfort and into operation despite cost.

The A. A. No. 6 left the dock of the Great Lakes Engineering Works in Detroit at 3:05 p.m. on January 15, 1917.

Shortly after leaving the dock she encountered heavy ice and became stuck fast at 6:30 p.m. the Tug Michigan was then called to her assistance and arrived at 9:10 a.m. the next day. Without too much trouble the tug was able to release her and start her on the way once more. The tug being discharged at 11:00 a.m.

Being in need of some minor repairs the A. A. No. 6 tied up at the Grand Trunk Elevator at Detroit for about two hours before proceeding across Lake St. Clair.

The ice on the lake was extra thick in places and the ship found the going tough, averaging a speed of about six miles an hour.

After crossing the lake she made good time all the way up around the dreaded southeast bend, blowing a salute as she passed old Joe Beddore, and stopped in the ice for the night just above Russell Isle at 8:10 p.m.

The next morning, January 17, she was underway again at 7:45 a.m. From there on her progress was slow as she ran into ice that was from 12 to 15 inches thick and heavily windrowed in places. Arriving at Port Huron she tied up for a short time to make repairs and adjust machinery. She left there at 4:35 p.m. for the long 240 mile run up Lake Huron to the Straits of Mackinaw. (She made the 70 mile trip from Detroit to Port Huron, stemming the current through blinding snow, heavy ice, and sub-zero weather, in about 13 hours actual running time and used around 100 tons of fuel.)

After leaving the blue-watered St. Clair River, steering N⅜E with Point Edward ranges over the stern, they passed Lexington and Sanilac making wonderful time on that fifty-six-mile stretch to Harbor Beach. While passing there at 11:00 p.m. they encountered a strong west wind that gradually shifted to the northwest with gale force and snow.

Being light, without cargo for ballast, they took a real beating that night while crossing Thunder Bay. At 10:30 a.m. the next morning the most welcome shadow of Thunder Bay Island appeared ahead through the flying spray and falling snow. Seeing this, they made a run for the shelter of the Island's north point.

Arriving there at 12:35 p.m. they hove to, let go both anchors and thus rode out the storm.

Late that evening the wind became puffy and after midnight started to die out. So at 4:35 a.m. they hove up and again headed for Mackinaw. Pounding along they passed Thunder Bay, Middle, and Presque Isle, Spectacle and Poe Reefs, and Cheboygan and Round Island lights. Making regular time they arrived at Old Mackinaw at 1:30 p.m. Here the ship was slowed by heavy ice about eighteen inches thick. The ice had piled up in places to a height of from twelve to fourteen feet. Meandering through these heavy floes, she kept working westward, passing the red light on St. Helena's Island at 2:45 p.m.

At 3:15 p. m. she fetched up standing in a field of heavy ice and refused to back up. After several attempts to shake her free it was decided to cease operations and the fires were banked for the night.

The next morning at 7 a.m. (January 20) all hands forward broke out their heavy weather gear and armed with ice spuds, bars and axes went over the side in an effort to spud her loose. While the engineers tried to loosen her by working the engines from full ahead to full astern, they also tipped her fore and aft by pumping water in and out of her forward and after holds. (This fore and aft tipping was also often done with short cargoes by running the cars up and down the car deck, and usually it proved to be very effective.)

She came loose at 3:30 p.m. and after turning around they headed back to Mackinaw City for assistance. (While turning here they broke some blades off the starboard wheel.) She arrived there at 5:15 p.m. and laid in the ice just off the city dock awaiting assistance from one of the carferries plying between upper and lower Michigan, from St. Ignace to Mackinaw City.

She laid at the dock all the next day (January 21) during a northeast gale with snow. While there, the crew dumped four hundred and fifty tons of fuel coal into her bunkers from the extra coal cars on her car deck.

At 6:45 a.m. on the twenty-second they left Mackinaw City to check over the ice conditions in the Straits. Finding them the same as before, they turned around at 8:00 a.m. and proceeded back to Mackinaw City.

Upon their return while working in the heavy ice off the city dock they stripped all four blades off the starboard wheel and broke the ends off all the blades on the port wheel. This left her almost helpless in the heavy ice that seemed to extend about twenty feet below the water line.

About noon of that day the Steamer Wawatan approached the scene to assist the A. A. No. 6 into St. Ignace, where they expected to tip up and replace the propeller blades. The Wawatan became stuck at 1:30 p.m. about two-hundred feet away from the A. A. No. 6. They then ran a line over to the A. A. No. 6, with which they were able to help loosen her by heaving on it at intervals with the windlass.

The Wawatan released herself at 4:30 p.m. and after breaking a wide channel for about a hundred feet she got stuck again and remained there for the night.

At 12:30 p.m. the next day the Wawatan broke herself loose and then, after breaking out the A. A. No. 6 at 2:00 p.m. she went ahead and made a channel for the disabled ship to follow. With just a few stubs left on her broken propellers the condition of the A. A. No. 6 was such that she could not get headway enough with which to steer and follow the channel, so she backed up to the city dock to await more assistance.

The Steamer Ste. Marie arrived at 10:00 a.m. on January 24 and taking the A. A. No. 6 in tow started across the Straits of Mackinaw to St. Ignace. Arriving there about noon they were tied up at the old lumber dock by 1:30 p.m. and preparations were made for tipping up the A. A. No. 6 to replace the broken propeller blades.

With the unfavorable ice conditions facing them it was a question of whether or not to leave the A. A. No. 6 at the dock until spring or try to proceed down the lake to Frankfort. So at

2:20 p.m. the Ste. Marie left for the Straits to check over the ice conditions, with Mr. Tousley and Mr. Osmer aboard representing the Ann Arbor Railroad.

Returning at 5:00 p.m. they agreed to try once more to reach the home port.

Late that afternoon the Steamer Ste. Marie ran her bow up to the stern of the A. A. No. 6 and after lining up their rails she unloaded the six empty fuel cars from the 6 and, returning to the slip. She exchanged them for six loaded ones that she placed aboard the A. A. No. 6 early the next morning. (These Mackinaw carferries were able to load or unload from the bow).

The crew then hove these cars up the tracks to her forward end. The weight of these cars tipped her bow down and stern up, exposing the hubs of her wheels enough to allow the engineers, working on planks off the ice, to replace the broken blades with new ones. Water ballast was also pumped into her forward holds to assist the tipping. While she was thus tipped, the crew replaced four blades on the starboard side and two on the port. This job was completed at 8:00 a.m. on January 27th. She then laid there to await assistance through the Straits.

With the Steamer Ste. Marie leading the way they started out at 6:00 a.m. on January 30th. Passing old Mackinaw Point at 7:30 a.m. they steered W½N heading for White Shoal light, just twenty miles away.

At 8:00 a.m. St. Helena Isle again bore abreast. Just after passing the island they encountered heavy ice, about eighteen inches thick, which was windrowed in places to over thirty feet in height. Through this they averaged three miles an hour for the balance of the afternoon and just before supper, while backing up, the starboard propeller was again damaged so they stopped for the night. They were then about two miles from White Shoal light.

On January 31st, they started up again at 6:30 a.m. and after running through heavy ice for about a mile and a half they could see with the aid of the ship's glasses, that the ice ahead was much thinner and without windrows. Seeing this, they decided to take aboard all the extra provisions that the Ste. Marie might have and finish the trip alone.

After blowing a salute to the Ste. Marie, the A. A. No. 6 headed clear of White Shoal through thin ice for the southward turn at Grays Reef about six miles ahead. Isle Aux Galets bore abeam at 10:30 a.m. from here they steered SW by S down the 65-mile stretch toward North Manitou Island. Finding little ice they hove abreast of Beaver Island at 1:15 p.m. and passed the Fox Island light at 3:20 p.m. Shortly after this they ran into some heavier ice and as the weather looked bad they decided to lie there until morning.

At 5:00 a.m. on February 1, they got underway again and headed southward from home. Passing the North Manitou Island Shoal light at 6:30 a.m. she pounded past Point Betsie at 9:00 sharp and blew into Frankfort harbor at 9:30 a.m. for the first time. The entire town turned out to welcome her.

As the A. A. No. 6 seemed to be built more full aft than the other ships in the fleet it was necessary to make some alterations at the slip before she could dock there. So they tied her up alongside the dock until she was able to enter the slip the next afternoon. Here the switch engine crew exchanged the empty fuel cars for loaded ones. After this the A. A. No. 6 left the slip and again tied up at the dock, where the crew once more made preparations for tipping her up to exchange the broken propeller blades. This was completed at 5:00 p.m. on February 5.

The first winter of her life, because of the heavy ice and bad weather, was really a tough one on the A. A. No. 6 used thirty-three propeller blades, (buckets) before spring. To overcome this the company had heavier one made and from then on she had no more trouble than the other boats. On April 2, 1917, all eight buckets were replaced by the crew, while tipped up in Frankfort, in 25 hours and 25 minutes.

On November 10th the No. 6 left Manistique at 4:00 a.m. The wind was light from the westward with a low hanging haze on the horizon. They were steering south on her regular gait until

7:20 a.m. when the wind with gale force and heavy snow tore out of the northwest. The No. 6 then made a wide-open run for the lee of South Manitou Island, arriving there at 2:00 p.m. Sheltered from the wind and sea, they ran her bow up on the sandy beach and weathered out the gale. The wind died out early the next morning and they backed her off and proceeded on their way.

Note: The sheltered shores of Lake Michigan's Manitou Islands have served as a harbor of refuge for over a hundred years. The lighthouse on the south island was built in 1839, being one of the oldest on Lake Michigan.

She left Frankfort on her first trip with cargo at 8:35 a.m. on February 6, 1917. the wind was south west, fresh and cloudy, and they steered W x S½S for Kewaunee, Wisconsin.

She arrived at Kewaunee at 1:25 p.m., but she did not fit into the slip very well she was delayed in tieing up. Her rails aft did not line up well with the rails on the apron and a car jumped the track while unloading. As very little damage was done, it was soon placed back on the rails. But when the first of the four strings of cars came aboard to load her, it left the rails on the stern in the starboard center and before it could be stopped did considerable damage to the boat. After leaving the track, these cars ran over the rudder post and into the after stanchion, fetching up there and breaking a hatch and damaging the emergency steering gear. This damage was later repaired at the shipyards at the expense of the insurance company.

(The months of January and February of this year, 1917, were one of the few times that Lake Michigan has ever been known to be frozen all the way across. This caused the boats to travel in pairs so as to be close by to assist each other through the bad spots enroute.)

When the A. A. No. 6 left Frankfort at 12:10 p.m. The wind was northwest, fresh, with snow flurries. They ran through light ice all the way over, arriving at Kewaunee, Wisconsin at 7:00 p.m. After exchanging cargoes they left there at 9:00 p.m.

heading for home. They made good time on their return trip until 1:00 a.m. the next day when they struck some heavy ice at full speed and became stuck fast in a windrow about thirty-five feet deep The No. 5 arrived at 3:00 a.m. to assist her and she also became stuck fast. At 1:00 p.m. that afternoon the No. 3 hove into sight from the westward and as the wind had shifted, which released the pressure on the ice, she was able to break the the No. 5 loose at 3:00 p.m. and she in turn broke out the No. 6.

Then with the "Bull of the Woods," as the A. A. No. 5 was often called, in the lead, they again headed for home single file, traveling through ice a foot thick. About two miles outside the harbor they hit some windrowed ice that was shoving. Seeing this, the A. A. No. 5 took a run at the harbor entrance with everything in her wide open. When about a mile outside she came to a dead stop and refused to back up. The No. 6 was right on her tail, and she also fetched up standing and stuck. The No. 3, struggling along in their channel, gradually came to a dead stop and ceased all operations.

The wind was west south west, strong and clear and being from this direction it kept shoving the ice in behind these imprisoned icebound ships, piling it up in places about thirty to forty feet high.

This made good sailing for the crews as most of them could walk ashore every day when off watch. They were icebound here until February 19, when the wind shifted and coming off land it released the pressure. This enabled the A. A. No. 4, which was then homeward bound from Manistique, to assist in breaking them out. They then proceeded to Frankfort without further incidence.

After the No. 5 had been handled inside, the No. 6 proceeded into the slip at 11:00 a.m., February 20, after having been gone over a week on that trip.

Bow of the A. A. No. 6 up to the stern of the A. A. No. 5 outside Frankfort (1917)

The A. A. No. 5 in dry docks Manitowoc. Pilot house of Arizona in foreground, Carolina in background.

The A. A. No.s 3, 6 and 5 outside Frankfort 1917

In 1917 Lake Michigan was all frozen over from February 12th to the 20th. In 1917 the A. A. No.s 5, 6 and 3 were stuck fast in rotation, just outside Frankfort. Paul Kirby, then driving for Geddes Livery Barn, transported crews and supplies on the ice with sleighs. They were intending to fuel up in this manner on Tuesday, February 20th, but the No. 4 came down from the northward in command of Capt. Charles Frederickson, Sunday, February 18th. The wind shifting, released some of the pressure on the ice, enabling the No. 4 to break out the No. 5. She in turn released the No.s 6 and 3.

During this tie-up a crew came out and tried to dynamite the A. A. No. 5 loose. The ice flew in all directions, one large piece coming down through the overhead of the No. 5's cabin. This has never been tried since.

On April 19th the A. A. No. 5 arrived at the Manitowoc Breakwater at 1:335 a.m. in a dense fog bound for the C.N.W.

slip. The wind was S. E. fresh. Slowly approaching the slip head on, it was found to be already occupied by the PM carferry No. 19. While cautiously crossing the 19's bow with intentions of tying up at the cheese dock they sighted more lights through the fog ahead. Which was the stern of the steamer Peter Riess unloading coal, at the Riess coal dock. While backing the A. A. No. 5 to clear the stern of the Riess, she fell down onto the rocky corner of the old Goodrich dock and broke off her starboard shaft, and bent the rudder stock. After the P.M. 19 left the A. A. No. 5 entered the slip unloaded and proceeded up the ship yards. She arrived in the dry dock at 2:00 p.m. May 9th and was ready for sea again on May 12th.

May 23rd--The A. A. No. 5 departed Frankfort 12:15 a.m. steering N. from Manistique, wind N.N.W. gale with snow. Hauled N½W at 2:15 a.m., hauled out N. again at 5:30 a.m. still snowing and glowing a gale. Picked up Point Au Barks 7:25 a.m. as it looked a little close they hauled out to E.N.E. after running this way for about 5 minutes the A. A. No. 5 struck the gravel bottom with a sudden lurch, but although she slowed and seemed to slide off sideways she kept on going and regained her headway, steering due east away from the land. Examination of her holds showed no apparent damage. After steering east for 15 minutes they again hauled north for Manistique and arrived there at 10:00 a.m. When she went to the dry dock in Manitowoc for hull inspection that fall on October 1st, it was found necessary to repair the brackets and skag, also replace some badly chipped buckets.

December 19th Trip 581. Departed Frankfort at 1:15 a.m. wind N.E. light and snowing hard. Steering N.W.½ W headed for the Door Passage enroute to Menominee. Stopped at 5:15 a.m. and picked up the white flash of Pilot Isle bearing N.N. E. Hauled out east and ran a few minutes and struck hard aft at 5:30 a.m. Let her run at full speed and she dug herself free and out into the deeper water. Looking over the stern they saw the red rings. on Plum Isle and lining them up came on through the pass safe. Again in the sounding of tanks and examination of bottom showed no damage.

The A. A. No. 5 was from Jan 31st to February 5th coming from Manistique to Frankfort and on trip no. 65 she was from February 27th to March 3, coming from Manitowoc to Frankfort. Often in these days of heavy ice fields they would follow a crack in the ice for miles and unless it carried them to far off their course they made fairly good time. When up around the islands in the north end of the lake they would see foxes, wolves and deer cross ahead of them.

Trip No. 229 - On June 28th the A. A. No. 5 departed Manitowoc at 1:45 a.m. steering N.E.xE.½E bound for Frankfort. With the wind S.E. moderate and heavy fog. Having not heard or seen a thing at 7:15 a.m. they checked down running under check for 5 minutes they stopped the engine at 7:20 a.m. intending to use the hand lead as soon as she lost her way, but at 7:25 a.m. she hit or slid up onto the sandy beach just 1 mile to the windward of south of the place. By working her from one hard over wheel to the other she started swinging and before they could get much water in her aft to tip her down by the stern she backed off by herself with no apparent damage and was soon on her way home.

Little did the crew of the A. A. No. 5 realize while sliding quietly into the piers of the home port of Frankfort at 5:45 a.m. on July 8th, 1918 that soon the most terrible and saddest accident involving the greatest loss of life ever to take place in the history of the Ann Arbor carferries. On this fatal day the A. A. No. 5 after arriving in the slip and exchanging cargos, by request of the chief engineer decided to lie in the slip and do some work on the boilers. At 9:40 a. m. while the engineers and after gang on watch were making these repairs a slip joint on the main steam line let go. The live steam escaping from here killed four men and badly scalded one other. On hearing their cries and the hissing of the escaping steam from where he stood watch on the car deck Lester Cooper, 2nd Mate then a young man, with a fair knowledge of the boiler and engine room(as he had in early years passed coal or worked in the after end), went down into the engine room and finding the proper valve shut off this destructing steam. Hook Fitzhugh said that it was a slip joint on the steam pipe between the two boilers on the starboard side that let go, and as Cooper had been fireman on her he shut off the main stop valve from the car deck.

While the visibility was clearing after the steam was shut off the switch engine came down and unloaded the boat. Making more room on the car deck in which to hoist the men up from the hold below. The dead were Lon Boyd, W. T, Archie Gailbraith 1st assistant, Arthur R. Gilbert coal passer and William Herbert Freeman 2nd engineer and the handyman that was also burned, name so far unknown.

Soon the whole town was in mourning and all flags floating at half mast. The following morning the steamship inspectors arrived to hold investigation covering the accident. While this was taking place, the A. A. No. 5 being a dead boat, having no steam was hauled out of the slip by lines and blocks and tied up at the dock. Where she remained until July 13th making repairs while the crew solomonly paid their respects to the former ship mates.

November 7th Trip 520 the A. A. No. 5 arrived in Manitowoc at 8:45 p.m. and because o f the false Armistice the crew celebrating up town held her up for 2 ½ hours after she was ready to go.

Four days later November 11th when news of the official Armistice came through, the A. A. No. 5 arrived again in Manitowoc at 7:35 a.m. moved out of the slip and tied up at the cheese dock at 10:00 a.m. while the entire crew went ashore to celebrate that the war was over at last. There were great doings up town and most ships had a facsimile of Old Kaiser Bill hanging in the foremast. At 3:35 a.m. the next morning after the last member of the crew had been carried or poured aboard, the A. A. No. 5 again put out to sea.

Trip 600 - December 10, 1918 As there was lots of heavy ice in the north end of the lake, the A. A. No. 4 and 5 were traveling in together and after waiting weather in Frankfort they decided to depart for Manistique as the wind seemed to get puffy. the A. A. No. 5 left there at 12:50 a.m. with the A. A. No. 4 as consort. steering N with the wind East, gale and snow flurries. Just outside the point they held up in ½ point to the eastward. They were abreast of the S. Manitou Isle at 2:55 a.m. and the North Isle at 4:00 a.m. Passing the North Isle, they worked away from the lee of the land and as they felt the large seas rolling from the eastward they hauled up N.N.E. to the S. Fox Isle. Approaching the Foxes they steered between them and headed into the Traverse Bay for shelter, with the A. A. No. 4 a short distance behind. Finding flat water abreast of Torch Lake they checked down and after she had lost her way let go the anchor, in 10 fathoms of water. This was at 1:15 p.m. the wind then was S.S.E and blowing a gale with heavy snow. At 3:30 p.m. that afternoon the sun started to peep through as there seemed to be a lull in the wind they hove up and got underway. Pass Grand Traverse Point at 4:10 p.m. and abreast of the N. Fox Isle at 5:50 p.m. Steering N.W ½ W Shortly after leaving the lee of the island they found a large sea still running and as it had set in thick again with falling snow they turned around and once more headed back for the shelter of the east shore. Not being able to hear or see a thing they checked down at 8:15 p.m. and at 8:20 p.m. they struck hard, pretty hard well aft. Much to their surprise she backed off and thinking that she was clear the Captain rung her up and headed out to sea steering W x N. She just started to gain good steerage way and fetched up standing at 8:35 p.m. She hit far enough forward this time to raise her bow out of the water. After filling her after compartments with water and tipping her down by the stern as far as they dared and swinging her with the wheel from hard over one way to the other, she slid off the bottom at 12:10 a.m. the next morning and again headed out into the lake. The A. A. No. 4 still following. While running under check the watch went down below and examined all the holds and found no leaks nor visible damage. Picking up the most welcome sight of Grand Traverse Point they ran it close to and hung off there in the lee. The wind was still

S.E. gale force and heavy snow. At 6:00 a.m. the wind started to moderate and soon they were under way out between the foxes headed for Manistique. They arrived there at 11:05 a.m. after spending 27 hours and 15 minutes in route, which is ordinarily a 7 hour run.

On January 3, 1918 the A. A. No. 6 left Manitowocc at 10:15 p.m. course E by N½N with the wind south, fresh and snowing. Without much headway left on her after creeping through miles of heavy slush ice, she reached open water and unexpectedly slid into the trough of a big dead swell from the southeast. This, before she could gather enough way to enable her to come up into the sea, rolled her over so deeply that she tipped over three large flat cars of square timbers on the car deck. As no one was injured, they left them as they were and headed for home arriving there at 5:00 a.m. on January 4. The section crew then came aboard and spent nineteen hours reloading the timbers before the rest of the cargo could be handled.

Years ago the shippers did not seem to understand that their freight might encounter some heavy weather while crossing the Lake and the cars were not loaded properly as they are today. Consequently, in the old days cars were dumped at sea, and often steel rails and other heavy material not made fast would come out through the side of the cars during a heavy roll. Today this seldom happens as the boats are equipped with all the latest aids to navigation and are able to hold up during bad weather and roll very little. Also cars that are considered rough loads are made fast before leaving port.

On January 30th beginning trip number 29, the A. A. No. 6 escorting the A. A. No. 4 left Frankfort at 9:00 p.m. bound for Manitowocc, Steering W by S½S with the wind northeast, fresh and snowing, they found the ice fairly light for about an hour. As they worked to the westward the ice became heavier and it started shoving shortly after midnight. At ten the next morning they took a run at a heavy windrow about two miles south of Two Rivers Point and became stuck fast. The A. A. No. 4 was also stopped about a mile to the southward, so the crew of the A. A. No. 6 walked over to the A. A. No. 4 and assisted them in spudding her loose.

The two crews working together released her at 5:30 p.m. on the 31st. The A. A. No. 4 then worked her way up to the A. A. No. 6 and broke her out at 7:00 p.m. The A. A. No. 6 then made a run for the harbor arriving there three hours later. Four hours after that, the cargoes having been handled they were on their way back to Frankfort. On the way they sighted the A. A. No. 5 and waited for her to pass so they could follow in her wake and make better time as she was by far the best ice-breaker in the fleet.

Nearing the harbor they sighted heavy ice piled up outside and after being stuck often they finally made the slip at 10:00 p.m. on February 3.

After she was loaded and ready to go they laid there until the morning of February 7 while the other boats battled the heavy ice in the harbor entrance. On her way out she became stuck fast between the piers. The A. A. No. 4 came back in and broke the ice all around her, but she still would not move. Later the A. A. No. 4 arrived and backing up to her stern lightened her up by taking off part of her cargo, but even then she refused to budge so they filled her up with water and let her set on the bottom overnight.

After pumping her out the next morning and with the A. A. No. 4 pulling on her tow line, she finally came loose at 9:00 a.m. on February 11.

A few hours after midnight the wind shifted to the southeast and as this was an offshore wind, it loosened the ice along the beach. When it grew light all, the boats went outside the harbor to check the ice conditions. As they still were bad they filled their drinking water tanks and went back inside for the night.

At nine the next morning the A. A. No. 5 left with R. H. Reynolds the marine superintendent aboard. The A. A. No. 4 following in her wake. After checking conditions at two hours out, Mr. Reynolds wired in for the other boats to proceed. So the A. A. No. 6 escorting the No. 3 left for Manitowoc at 11:30 a.m. on February 13. Strange as it may seem the boats were bothered but very little with ice during the rest of the winter.

On June 8, 1919 when a tug was winding the Str. Christopher Columbus around in Milwaukee harbor, her long narrow bow overlapped the dock, knocking the legs out from under a large water tank. Capt. Moody jumped off the flying bridge to safety with the wheelsman under his arm just as the tank lit where hey had been standing. Eighteen people were killed by this falling tank.

October 27, 1919, the A. A. No. 3 was caught in a N.E. gale and snow, which shifted to the westward while coming home from Death Door, and but for the brave crew, the cook and the good seamanship of the Captain B. H. Hansen of Manitowoc, she would have foundered and caused the Indian Drum to beat again. She had almost a full cargo of lumber on this trip and sure was a sorry sight when she arrived at Frankfort. There were cars hanging over her stern, lumber all over her decks, some sticking out through port holes and her main steam pipe leading forward was broken, frames and stanchions bent and ripped out also several cars off the track.

The Christopher Columbus, was built for the World's Fair in 1892, ran 21 miles per hour, was 362 feet long, 42 foot beam, of 1511 gross tons and carried as high as 6500 passengers. Like so many other gallant ships of her day was scrapped in 1936 at Manitowoc for $3,500, though it cost $200,000 to build her.

October 28, 1919 while the A. A. No. 4 was on the Grand Haven to Milwaukee run, she got caught in a real old time gale from the westward. It took her 27 hours to cross the lake. Her schedule dtime in flat water being 6 hours. This same trip she met the Crosby Line Str. City of Muskegon, going east to her doom. (she foundered at Muskegon, loss of 29 lives. Some bodies were picked up 6 miles north of there on November 14th).

This was a bad blow on the lakes, with a loss of 19 ships and 75 sailors.

November 6, 1919. While running through the Sturgeon Bay canal at 1:30 p.m. east bound, under check the A. A. No. 5 parted the lines and set adrift the steamer Manchester and consort tow, the old now converted once great sailing ship of the sea Oak Leaf. They were tied up there because of bad weather outside.

February 23, 1920. In addition to her regular cargo on this trip the A. A. No. 5 took aboard a carload of hay and other small supplies for the 200 starving head of cattle and hungry islanders on the North Manitou Isle. She also had on board the Assistant Light keeper and his wife from the South Isle. She left Frankfort at 6:37 a.m., with the wind N.W. and clear and headed for the islands. When about one hour out they received a message on the wireless to proceed more to the westward and release the south bound the A. A. No. 4 who was stuck fast in the ice west of the south island. As her hull hove into sight they steered on it, as this changed their course they knew that she was free and again headed for the islands. After being stuck in the heavy ice twice the A. A. No. 5 arrived off the south end of the North Isle and when within 1/4 of a mile of the beach at 1:00 p.m. they stopped and as there was no sign of life on the island the Captain, sent the mate and one of the sailors ashore to notify the islanders that they were there. At 4:00 p.m. they returned with several men, horses and sleighs. The supplies were unloaded at 5:00 p.m. and they got underway heading for the South Island. The mate said that on the N. Island several of the cattle were dead and that their hides had been removed and were spread out over stumps. The A. A. No. 5 having stopped in ice between the island for the night, arrived off the south island at 6:30 a.m. The next day and sent the Keeper and his wife ashore over the ice. After dodging heavy ice fields all the way, the A. A. No. 5 arrived at Manistique at 8:30 p.m. the evening of February 24th.

Arriving at Frankfort on March 3rd at 11:40 a.m., the A. A. No. 5 found the harbor full of boats and the entire Railroad at a standstill because of a snow and sleet storm from the N.W. on March the 11th. As there was still no movement on the railroad the crews of all the boats joined the section crews and went out on the right of way to shovel now. They left at 7:00 a.m. and returned that evening at 6:30 p.m. and only got as far as Copemish. On the 14th the north bound train got through to Frankfort and on the 15th the A. A. No. 5 was loaded. She then left the slip and broke out the A. A. No. 4 and that had become frozen in during the cold days while lying still in the harbor awaiting a cargo. the A. A. No. 5 finally left Frankfort at 2:00 p.m. that afternoon bound for Manitowoc.

At 5:00 p.m. March 24, 1920 the A. A. No. 4 left for Manitowoc. Wind east strong and dense fog. While running under check and listening for the foghorn, she hit a large boulder that poked a hole in her, under the boilers. The king mate, known as 'Liverpool Al', was then on the forecastle deck and right after she hit, he sang out to the captain that he could hear the fog horn. They rang her up for all she had, making a dash for the harbor. Tying up at the old Goodrich Co. dock just as she nestled on the bottom in about 20 feet of water. They pumped her out and after unloading the cargo took her upriver to the shipyards..

She was back in service again April 14, 1920.

While the A. A. No. 4 was in Manistique for cargo early in the morning on October 28th we saw the schooner Rosabelle, with her long whiskered crew, lying there windbound.

On our return trip to Frankfort we received orders to proceed to Grand Haven under charter for 10 days to the Grand Truck R.R.

October 31, 1921 about noon, while on the Grand Haven to Milwaukee run the A. A. No. 4 sighted a wooden hull floating bottom side up. This was just after a two day blow from the N.E. the A. A. No. 4 checked down, drifting alongside. We were 40 miles out of Milwaukee.

The 2nd Officer, O. B. Olson, who could recognize anything carrying canvas, after squinting his weather eye over the rail, faced the wind, lighted his old corn cob pipe saying, "She is the Rosabelle out of Benton Harbor."

The schooner Rosabelle was a two master of 131 gross tons. Built in 1873. Formerly of Sheboygan, Wisconsin sold to the House of David in Benton Harbor.

After wiring the Coast Guard at Milwaukee we cruised around for a while under check, in hopes of finding some sign of her crew, but to this day none were ever found.

The Rosabelle was bound for Benton Harbor, Michigan with a load of lumber from High Isle in the north end of Lake Michigan, which at this time was part of the kingdom, under the jurisdiction of King Ben Parnel and Queen Mary, rulers of the House of David colony out of Benton Harbor. The Kingdom was broken up during a long trial in 1927. A band of wild horses is the only sign of life on this Isle today seen by fisher folk while passing with the Isle close aboard.

Later we heard that the U. S. Cutter "Tuscorara" had steamed hurriedly to our given position and after cruising around all day did not find a sign of the old Rosabelle.

The Schooner Rosabelle foundered in Lake Michigan, October 30, 1921, and the Steamer Rising Sun
4 went on the beach with 5,000 bushels of potatoes aboard at Good Harbor, during an old time three day Nor'wester in November 1918 and is still there.

Wreck of Rosabelle in Racine, Wisconsin

March 15th 1921, the A. A. No. 5 with a full load left
Frankfort north bound for Manistique at 2:45 a.m. steering N ½
E. The wind was east moderate with light rain. After steering
this course for 6 hours 8:45 a.m. and not being able to pick up
any sight of the land they hauled out to N.E. Although they could
see about a mile they checked down at 9:05 a.m. and after she lost
her headway they took a cast with the hand lead and got 16 fathom
of water under her and hauled back into N.N.E. still running
under check and listening for the fog horn. Coming to a stop for
another cast at 9:30 a.m. they got six fathoms and hauled out to
due S. Not hearing anything at 10:05 a.m. and taking another cast
the lead showed 8 fathoms. While steering this course and
running at half speed, the A. A. No. 5 fetched up standing at
10:40 a.m. as after while the crew was taking soundings around
her hull the wind shifting the westward cleared up the fog and they
found that they were on the dreaded rocky spot called Wiggens
reef which is located off Wiggens Point and about 6 miles south

of Manistique. After filling up and pumping out the holds in an effort to tip her fore and aft and by working the wheels full speed in both directions she started to swing on a hard over wheel about a quarter of a point at 2:00 p.m. and at 6:00 p.m. she was swinging over a point and swinging this on a hard over wheel she backed off at 8:20 p.m. and they steered out East for 15 minutes and then headed for the harbor steering N x E. Arriving there at 9:10 a.m. While in the slip and exchanging cargos the watch checking all the holds could find no leaks so after loading they proceeded to Frankfort. After running until March 28th when the ship yard found room in the dry dock they entered the yard and found it necessary to take off and reroll ten bottom plates and repair both of here sleeves. She put to sea again on April 8th.

In 1922, the A. A. No. 3 went into the ship yard at Manitowocc, she was placed in the dry dock and cut in two. The sections of the deck were then spread apart and a third section was placed in the middle, upon which a new piece 48 feet long was built and spliced into the middle of the A. A. No. 3, lengthening her hull from 258 feet to 306 feet with the same beam.

Finding the ice well windrowed near Sherwood Point, the A. A. No. 5 leaving Menominee at 2:10 p.m. on January 2, 1922 decided to make the return trip to Frankfort by way of Death Door Passage. Arriving outside at 4:00 p.m. they found a big southerly sea in the lake with snow and turned around. After dropping the anchor in 20 fathoms of water in Hedge Hog Harbor they rode out the gale. The wind shifted to the westward during the night and they got under way again early the following morning. Arriving in Frankfort at 6:00 p.m. on January 3rd. Although there was no mention of a grounding during this anchorage in the blinding snow storm, the A. A. No. 5 went to the ship yard at Manitowoc on January 7th and was still there during the great sleet storm of February 22, 1922. While there she replaced the port shaft and wheel and also shipped a new rudder.

February 22, 1922 was the year of the big sleet storm. The worst ever in Benzie county. All boat and railroad service was at

97

a standstill for about a week. The A. A. No. 4 came over from Manitowoc in this storm. Mr. Harry Sutter was aboard. He being chief steward of the line rode with us often. We always looked forward to this as he was a past master at story telling.

This morning the galley with the gang gathered around he was in the middle of a yarn about a little Swede taking a big Norwegian into camp when the A. A. No. 4 took a side sliding deep roll that brought the sleet laden after spar crashing down overhead. We never did hear the finish of that story. Next trip we went to the yard and stepped a new spar.

May 10, 1922 with the wind easterly and heavy fog the A. A. No. 4 piled up on Green Isle the second time. While there a gravel scow came out inquiring if any assistance was needed. The good-humored captain said he had intended to await high tide but that the scow might give a demonstration, which she did, and to the great surprise of all hands the A. A. No. 4 was released with no damage.

On June the 15th as the A. A. No. 5 was west bound through the Sturgeon Bay Canal, the usual sight seeing crew on deck witnessed the Historical Breakwater jumping Schooner "Mary Ellen Cook," being pushed into her final resting place at the golf grounder at 10:15 a.m. She was to be used as a swimming dock for the public. Later she was burned up and the remaining scrap iron sold for junk. On this trip as the A. A. No. 5 continued on through the Sawyer, Sturgeon Bay bridge they saw the old three master the J.H. Stevens, sunk with a hole in her side, just off the ship yards as the result of a collision of the day before. On entering the harbor of Frankfort at 10:20 a.m. on July 10, 1922, the A. A. No. 5 seeing the lumber barge Spokan on the beach just south of the place came about and asked them if they needed any assistance. The Spokan said that they would be able to get off by themselves so the A. A. No. 5 proceeded on into the harbor. The wind was from the eastward and hazy. Later the same day the Spokan backed off and went on her way.

November 14, 1922 the A. A. No. 4 left Frankfort bound

for Manitowoc. The wind kept slowly increasing from the southward, reaching gale force about 5 hours out. The seas grew higher and longer, then finally three mountainous ones came along together. She lifted her proud bows ladylike over the first sea, met the second one with such terrific force that she lost most of her way, dipping her stern entirely under the last one, shipping solid blue water her entire length. These deep side twisting dives started two strings of her cargo running fore and aft. The only way to refasten these cars was to smooth the water by bringing her around, with the sea behind her. After refastening the cargo the Old Man decided to look for shelter. The seas were too big to make Kewaunee or the Sturgeon Bay canal so we made a run for Death Door passage.

After entering the shelter of the Door we hauled to the southward heading for Sturgeon Bay. Approaching the canal from the westward we found the rest of the Ann Arbor fleet tied up here for weather. This was the intention of the A. A. No. 4 but while passing them under check some skipper yelled over in a sarcastic tone of voice asking how the weather was outside. The old man, having been up all day and not in the best of humor, answered "Why don't you follow us and find out?" So at full speed ahead we went to sea again combing the beach we finally arrived at Manitowoc, having completely circumnavigated the upper part of Door County Wisconsin, traveling about 259 miles without stopping the engines for nearly 30 hours.

On the night of her departure while loading in Frankfort the air was very still, no wind and a light crisp snow. Standing on her stern awaiting cargo one could hear the pins fall in the bowling alley across the bay.

On December 16th while the A. A. No. 5 was on her way to Menominee and passing through the west end of the canal she found the channel blocked by the little Hooker Kina. Which was suck fast in the heavy ice. the A. A. No. 5 was delayed an hour here while breaking her load and digging a channel around her.

The A. A. No. 5 in Frankfort (Elberta Slip) Lucia Simpson in harbor right, Str. Manitou at North Michigan dock, small dot approaching large slip is bell ferry. They docked in Elberta side at dock in foreground, wooden walkway alongside boat.

This narrative of the A. A. No. 4 is written in commemoration of the brave hearts within the seafaring folks, living, drowned or dead, that so heroically endeavored to keep her afloat during times of stress when she put forth her every effort, particularly when she foundered on February 14, 1923.

She left Frankfort on February 13, 1923 at 8:15 p.m. wind easterly, light, with snow. Course WxS1-4S bound for Kewaunee, Wisconsin, which was a 5 hour run in ordinary weather. Sigrud Frey who was relieving went ashore and the captain (Old Man) came aboard. The A. A. No. 4 took on nineteen cars of cargo, consisting of 17 cars of coal, 1 auto and 1 salt.

While in the pilothouse, being on watch at the wheel from 6 to 10 with Randall Plant the 3rd Officer, we noticed that about 9:30 p.m. a sort of pressure on our ear drums and that our voices seemed to echo inside our heads. The wind came when the two hands of the clocks were together at 10 minutes to 10:00 p.m. It brought no sea with it as is often the case, but it was not long in making, being almost ahead, from the W.N.W. It grew colder and colder. Coming off watch at 10:00 p.m. I went to bed but not for long. Soon Bost 4 was being tossed about like a toy. No one needed to be called as she herself took care of that.

The wind blowing a living gale of about 80 miles per hour. whipped the lake in a fury and soon the waves were 30 feet high. The mercury went down to 22° below zero. The plight of crew, ship and cargo became very serious as the cars between decks soon broke loose from the rails. Some of the cars started running up and down the deck with the rise and fall of her hull. One car of autos went out the stern into the open sea. Taking the protection of the old wooden sea gate along. Two heavy coal cars went halfway over the stern and hung there. Much to the surprise of everyone they were still there in the spring when they raised her. Liverpool Al and his gang dumped the contents of some coal cars overboard. this would cause a big list and in such a seaway soon roll her over. One coal car was off the track just over the engine room on the port side. It was tipped over, outboard, and one of its wheels against the release valve on the low pressure cylinder, sliding up and down as she rolled. If this valve was broken it would cause the port engine to stop and Bost 4 in this sea with one engine could not live long. the chief engineer with part of the crew and the aid of chains and turnbuckles soon heaved it to one side.

101

It looked as though everyone was busy everywhere and for a while it seemed like there were broken jacks, chains and top hooks together with bent stanchions and lumps of coal flying all around. There were some cars madly racing fore and aft in the port center from the forward bumping post to the derailed cars aft. Orastus Kinney and I decided we would stop this by catching these cars with end jacks when they fetched up at the bumping post. He broke his thumb and I awoke partly submerged under coal that fell off the car as it listed toward me during the few seconds that the jack held before flying apart. While Capt. Ole was looking over my broken hand we saw the old man step across from one coal car to another with a rail clamp in each hand on his way forward in the starboard wing. These clamps weighed about 75 lbs. apiece and were very awkward to carry. He certainly did his share and seemed to be everywhere.

While James Dorey, the boss porter, was applying first aid in the galley and some of the boys had negligently gathered around the Old Man stuck his face and pipe inside the door, saying, "Boys, I have taken you to sea for a good many years, always bringing you safely home, and will do it this time if only you will give us a badly needed hand." So down between decks we went again, cold, hungry, banged heads, broken bones and all.

Ed Gabrielson and Nils (Bo) Dropping were considered the best men ever to work on a car deck at this time and this story would be incomplete without a mention of the great effort they put forth this night.

'Tis hard for one working on the decks above to describe and give proper credit to the brave engineers, oilers and firemen that did so heroically keep her afloat and her machinery operating. the fact that she did survive and pass up the ever inviting hospitality of Davy Jones is proof that they stuck to their posts to the last man.

At 1:00 a.m. the seas became so big and the wind so strong that Boat 4 trying her very best could not keep her proud bows facing it any longer. So rolling her rails under and shipping cold blue water her entire length as the mountainous seas came aboard taking part of her rails off the main deck with them, she came around, loosening everything solid aboard her, including the smoke stack which was soon made fast with gear from the car deck. While coming around she laid broadside in this big sea for at least 20 minutes before she made up her mind to put the sea behind her and head for home, rolling as no boat ever rolled before or since. In her crippled condition with very little headway and half full of water, 'tis just a miracle that she ever came out of it.

During this time all anyone could do was to hang on with a prayer and watch things smash to pieces, tearing all her side center stanchions loose, causer her upper deck to raise and fall with the sea which caused the steam pipe to the big whistle to break off flush with the deck. The chief engineer crawled on top of the boilers, which was a very dangerous place to be, and shut off the valve, thus saving the escaping steam which was so vital to Boat 4.

After she came around things went along much better as she did not roll so deep. But it was very heartrending to watch the big sea, that often came aboard her open stern and to know that the water was slowly but surely gaining on her pumps, thus realizing that it was only a matter of time for us all.

About 5:00 a.m. McKesson, the purser, sent the S.O.S. and around 6:30 a.m. he informed us that we must be quite close to Frankfort as the radio signal was very strong. This made us all feel better knowing we were nearing land but of course this did not answer the all important question as to where we would finally fetch up, which meant everything in this seaway.

In the pilothouse they were discussing this same question, the second mate O.B. Olsen said he believed she was heading about on Point Betsie. Someone else agreed with him. A third party thought she was too far to the southward, but the Old Man with his pipe going strong said, "We won't change her course' and to Peter Storm, the wheelsman, "Steady as you go." Being so cold it was very thick with steam on the water and one could only see about a boat length.

On Valentine Day, February 14th at 7:00 a.m. just after daylight we heard the most welcome sound of the fog horn and at the same time saw the south pier dead ahead. The Old Man ordered the wheel "Hard left" in an effort to swing her clear of the pier and into the harbor entrance, but as the Boat 4 was almost full of water and carrying the heaviest part of her cargo aft she was way down by the stern. Her draft being about 18 feet instead of the usual 13 feet. So when about one half length away from the pier she dropped down between two big seas and fetched up aft. This tore her complete wheel and shaft off on the starboard side and also broke the rudder stock. When she came up on the next sea, she fetched up standing against the N.W. corner of the south pier with such force it was hard to keep your feet. This knocked off a large ice encased portion of the pier. It was then that the merciless seas of cold blue water rolled in her open stern filling her completely with water and ice just as the crew climbed out of her hold. the quiet spoken, never idle, chief engineer being last, coming up the stairway with the sea knee-deep behind him.

She swung to the northward laying broadside across the pier. Pounding against it just aft of the bluff of the starboard bow, the sea and wind hammering on her port, bow slowly broke her around the end of the pier heading her into the channel where she came to rest about half a length inside, against the south pier. She started to list badly to port and some of the boys began to string a line outside the rail fore and aft so they could stay on the high side if she tipped over but the Old Man stopped this saying "She won't roll over." Soon she righted herself to an even keel and settled down fairly well except now and then a big sea would roll in, raise her up against the pier with a bang, then let her fall back on the bottom.

The Coast Guard came out on the walk of the north pier with their breeches bouy, but the Old Man waved them back. Soon she quieted down and laid close enough to the pier so that we could put a ladder over. The rope line, called boat falls, was brought down from the boat deck and it was agreed that we would all take hold of this as we went over the side traveling single file. In case one of us fell down he would have something to hang onto and the rest could hold him up. This worked out fine and the boys picking up what clothing they could find started over the side but the Old Man didn't want to leave saying, "She has been a faithful old girl, bringing us all back home, so I guess I will stick around and see how she lays her." We refused to go without him. He was almost asleep setting in the corner of the wheelhouse bench. When he saw that we intended to stay, he came along real mad, with his eyebrows sticking straight out (which was always a sign of his anger).

This stepping down upon the wide, easy walking breakwater into the arms of waiting friends, as it was stated in many of the papers at this time was not all true. The entire length of the sea wall was a solid mass of ice. Built up in forms of volcanic craters by the big seas rolling in, often with such force it would dash skyward for 25 or 30 feet, freezing as it fell. the only way one could walk was to meander around and follow the narrow shoreward run of these spray flying, sea roaring craters. Tired, hungry, and half frozen as everyone was, it was just an act of God that kept some of the boys from falling in, which would have meant instant death. But everyone made it ashore and safely home.

Most of the boys were frozen in some part of their bodies. The clothes they wore made them odd looking characters. The big Hindu had at least three bed sheets and two blankets tied around his person, but still his hands and ears were frozen. emil Jonson walked down that cold windswept beach to his home in Arcadia, some seven miles away.

Thus ended the sinking of the A.A. No. 4 'Twas only by the Grace of God she ever lived to tell the tale, having much better luck than other ships in her trade. The new carferry Marquette and Bessemer sank in a big blow on Lake Erie in 1909 with the loss of 36 lives.

The A. A. No. 4 alongside pier

Car deck the A. A. No. 4 showing tipped over cars and damaged stanchions.

The A. A. No. 5 alongside removing car from the A. A. No. 4

Building Coffer Dam on the A. A. No. 4

The first Pere Marquette No. 18 left Milwaukee bound for Ludington on September 8, 1910. She shank enroute off Port Washington, Wisconsin being a total loss and drowning about half her crew.

The carferry Milwaukee sank in the open sea off Racine in October 1929. She took 51 sailors and the cook along. She was built in 1903, painted all white and was called the Manistique. While they were building the new slip in Northport, Michigan for the Manistique run, she used to trade into Frankfort, Kewaunee and Manitowoc. She was a nicely built boat but never had much power.

The rest of the fleet, including the Pere Marquette No. 17, which was rented to replace the A. A. No. 4, kept in operation all winter, except when large westerly seas caused them to hang off under the Wisconsin shore.

The experiments made at this time between Samp Slyfield, chief operator of the Elberta hill station and (Mac) Ferris McKesson, purser of the A. A. No. 4, which greatly assisted her in finding the nearness of the harbor, later developed into our present day Direction Finders, which today are one of the most useful aids known to navigation.

This was also the winter of the big snow. The boats made two trips during this storm. The entire fleet and railroad were tied up from March 19th to April 4th.

The crew of the A. A. No. 4 with the crews of all the fleet went out on a work train to shovel snow. When the train got stuck all hands would go over the side and shovel her loose.

The Reed Wrecking Co. from Port Huron, Michigan, came up with their large tug and scows to raise the A. A. No. 4.

During the time the A. A. No. 4 was resting on the bottom and partly blocking the harbor entrance following the disaster in February 1923, the A. A. No. 5 was used as a lighter, which a large crane on her car deck. (as can been seen in the picture). When ever the weather would permit the A. A. No. 5 would go outside and come to an anchor and after dropping down stern to the A. A. No. 4 would use the crane to hoist out the cars aboard the stern of the sunken the A. A. No. 4. Some of these she did save and others were just towed out into the deeper water and left there.

The first step was to send out the A. A. No. 5 with a big crane aboard to pick up the coal cars on her fantail, making room in which to build the necessary coffer dam across her open stern.

When this dam had been built and the diver had been down to plug up all the leaks including a large six foot hole in her starboard side which was caused by her riding the swell that ground her against the rip rap at the end of the pier, they proceeded to pump her out.

The coffer dam was completely washed out on March 16th and all work on her came to a standstill with any westerly weather. the A. A. No. 3 assisting the tug on their attempt finally pumped her out and towed her into the harbor on May 21, 1923.

She laid at the dock here making repairs until May 25th. the A. A. No. 5 using the tug Arctic astern towed her to Manitowocc shipyards on May 26th. Here she was completely overhauled and had all new cabins built on her main deck. She was back in service again on October 7, 1923.

While the A. A. No. 4 was in the yard in 1923 the Goodrich Co. borrowed the Old Man to sail their Steamer Arizona which was then on the Chicago, Green Bay and Menominee run. She carried passengers and package freight.

The Str. Arizona, like several other once proud ships of the sea that have outlived their usefulness, and perhaps 'tis best to say just gone as so few know where and care less, lays with her main deck mostly awash moored in the mud of the Old Maumee river at Toledo, Ohio, just through the Ash street bridge starboard side to inbound.

Also during the big freeze and sleet with snow storm during the month of March the crew of the A. A. No. 5 also went out on the railroad and shoveled the snow on the main line.

The A. A. No. 5 departed Frankfort at 2:11 a.m. north

109

bound for Manistique on April 7th. The wind was slightly fresh with light snow. She steered her regular course of N ½ E until abreast of the North Manitou Isle and as they found large fields of shifting ice they found it necessary to alter the course many times while dogging around them and trying to stay in the open water. After being out 5 hours the wind shifted to the eastward and it set in snowing. Soon the wind increased to gale force but as the north end of the lake was full of ice it did not make much sea except in the large open spots. In the old days before the radar and direction finder and gyro on trips like this one when the course was so often changed dodging ice ahead, the boat sometimes found it necessary to crack up in some extra heavy fields of ice and either go around it or take a second run in an effort to break through and it became almost impossible for the navigating officer to plot his correct position by judging his time and speed. Especially in a blinding snow storm and gale of wind. So at noon not having heard anything they checked down and made a cast with the hand lead, and finding six fathoms of water they steered to the northward under slow speed and stopped once more at 1:00 p.m. for another sounding and finding only three fathoms and rung her up headed out into the lake steering E.S.E. While swinging around here, sort of slowed and fetched up well aft but did not stop. As she was swinging at the time on a hard over wheel she seemed to slide off sideways and kept on heading out to sea. Not being able to find any sign of leaks or damage they headed out into the lake for ½ hour, and then N. again. At 4:00 p.m.. as the lead showed no bottom, they again got under way and as the snow let up enough to see a couple of miles they let her run at full speed until they sighted the land at 5:45 p.m. and arrived at the breakwater at 6:00 p.m. It was tough according to here time that she struck bottom near Pt. Aux Bauques which lays south of Manistique.

In 1924 on November 28th with the wind S. E. fresh and foggy, the A. A. No. 4 piled up on the beach just north of Kewaunee, Wisconsin. She backed off by herself while riding the swell in about three hours. No apparent damage at this time.

The A. A. No. 3 after she was lengthened and remodeled. Notice her new after pilot house (1923)

The A. A. No. 4 turning around in Frankfort harbor after her rebuilding in 1924

The A. A. No. 4 and 5 breaking ice in Green Bay, March 1, 1924

The A. A. No. 6 left Frankfort bound for Sturgeon Bay canal on December 3, 1924 with the wind west northwest, strong and clear, with a dead south swell. About nine miles off the Wisconsin shore she sighted a steamer flying distress signals. Coming closer they found her to be the Steamer Lakeland, owned and operated by the Thompson Transit Company.

The A. A. No. 6 stood by and picked up her crew of 27 persons as they cam alongside in four life boats. Later these life boats were taken over by the Coast Guard and towed to Sturgeon Bay Canal where they laid on the beach for many months.

The Lakeland, commanded by Captain NcNeely, was engaged in carrying automobiles between Detroit, Cleveland, Milwaukee, and Chicago. Headed for Chicago, with a load of Rickenbacker automobiles from Detroit she had laid windbound at the canal the night before and put to sea the next day, December 3. After being out about one hour she was found to be in a leaking condition and the captain hauled her about and headed back for the canal, but she made water so rapidly that soon the fires were out and she started to settle by the stern. By the time the A. A. No. 6 arrived she was in a sinking condition and had been abandoned by her crew.

Steamer Lakeland

The Lakeland sank stern first in 36 fathoms of water and the force of the imprisoned air in her hull trying to escape blew her hatches and cabin skylights high in the air just before she submerged at 11:25 a.m.

The insurance company before making the payment of $116,800 to the owners, started an investigation of the disaster. During August in 1925 they brought up a diving barge and five divers from New York. These deep sea divers went down to the Lakeland and looked her over.

The case was tried in Cleveland by the Federal Court in October 1925, but the jury could reach not agreement. Another trial was held in February 1926 and was settled in favor of the owners.

The Lakeland was built in Cleveland in 1887. She was 280 feet long with a 40 foot beam.

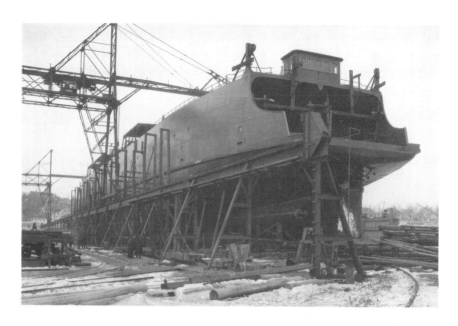

The A. A. No. 7 on stocks before her launching

Launching of the A. A. No. 7

The A. A. No. 7 early in her life

The A. A. No. 7 was built at the ship yards in Manitowoc, Wisconsin at the cost of about one miilion dollars. She was launched with a large celebration at 2:00 p.m. on January 2, 1925.

The A. A. No. 7 was built along the same lines as the Strs. Per Marquette Nos. 21 and 22 except they have straight stems and that of the A. A. No. 7 is well cut away.

She is 347.9 ft. long, 52 ft beam and has a depth of 19.2 ft. She carries an average load of 26 box cars. This also leaves room for about 8 or 10 autos. Her tonnage being 2,934 gross and her deep draft amidships 14' 11¼". The overhead clearance on the cargo deck is 15' 6." Her average speed is 14.5 miles per hour.

Besides the 12 modern commodious staterooms she has a large spacious cabin, observation and smoking room, also a beautiful dining room finished in natural grained light oak seating 35 people, with large windows along the outboard side, which affords a pleasant view of all passing scenery.

After leaving the ship yards she docked at the Soo and Chicago Northwestern slips where they loaded on a full cargo. She then put to sea on her maiden voyage, departing from Manitowoc breakwater at 7:18 a.m. on February 22 and arriving at Frankfort at 12:45 p.m. the same day, making this 75 mile run in 5 hrs and 27 min.

February 13, 1925 the A. A. No. 4 again made the beach just north of Kewaunee. The wind was N.E., fresh and foggy. She fetched up on Sunday afternoon at 5:30 p.m. The str. Pere Marquette No. 19 had just gone inside ahead of her, having much better luck in catching a clear spot in the fog.

The A. A. No. 3 came over from Frankfort, checked down, came up into the wind, dropped her hook and backed down to the A. A. No. 4. After passing her towing hawser the A. A. No. 3 pulled on the A. A. No. 4, Monday until noon, with no results.

The A. A. No. 3 then went inside the slip in Kewaunee, here she unloaded about half her cargo, the two center strings of cars. She then returned to the A. A. No. 4, backing down to her stern to stern. After being made fast to each other the crew filled the vacant space of the shelf pieces with wooden blocks, ties, etc. They then evened up their cargo decks by filling the after compartment of the A. A. No. 3 with water.

Eight cars of cargo from the A. A. No. 4 were then transferred over to the center tracks of the A. A. No. 3 with the aid of her capstans. This shifting of cargo of course lightened up boat 4 considerably.

After casting off all lines and again making fast the towing hawser, the A. A. No. 3 worked slowly ahead pulling the A. A. No. 4. She had more success this time and floated her free at 12:30 a.m. Tuesday.

She then went inside and unloaded the balance of her cargo in Kewaunee. After checking her over for leaks, etc., the A. A. No. 4 proceeded south to the shipyards at Manitowoc, arriving there February 15, 1925.

116

After a complete overhauling she was heady for sea again on April 5, 1925.

During the years from 1926 to 1936 the A. A. No. 4 was laid up (out of service) at different times in Frankfort harbor. Being placed in operation at various periods whenever the balance of the fleet could not handle the excess cargo.

In 1937 the State of Michigan purchased her to carry passengers and autos across the Straits of Mackinaw.

During June 1937, Capt. Sigrud M. Frey, then working for the state, came down from Mackinaw to sail the A. A. No. 4 with Len Swiger as chief engineer. On June 10, with a skeleton crew aboard, she bid her last farewell to the peaceful waters of Betsie Bay and headed again for the shipyards at Manitowoc. here she was placed in the dry docks for a complete checking over and her entire white works were sand blasted, having rusted badly while out of service. She left the yards August 1st bound for Cheboygan Michigan, where she laid for six weeks while they tore up her tracks and prepared her cargo deck for the auto traffic. She was then placed in service here and has been to this day complete success in her trade. In 1948 she went to the shipyard at Detroit and had her forward end remodeled so that she could take on cargo and cars at either end.

Just after the big blow from the NW on October 17, 1925 while enroute from Death Door Passage to Menominee, Michigan. the A. A. No. 7 passed a large raft of drifting logs, close aboard on the port side. This was two miles NNE of Chambers Isle in Green Bay. They reported this to the Coast Guard who immediately sent a tug in search of it. This was probably one of the last of the many large log booms, which in the days of old, were towed for miles across our lakes and bays to the nearest saw mills. They were a menace to navigation, particularly after dark and during thick weather. Capt. Dan Seavy, like many others when making port during bad weather, demanding lots of speed and carrying perhaps too much canvas, would often use these log booms, inside, to a good advantage by heading her into one while

117

he shortened sail. As she pounded her way over these logs they acted as a brake and gradually took the way off her.

In the cargo loaded aboard the A. A. No. 6 at Manistique on April 6, 1926 were two box cars filled with badly needed supplies for the icebound people on North Manitou Island. the A. A. No. 6 left Manistique at 1:35 a.m. with the wind west and clear, steering south, then at 4:30 a.m. they hauled southeast for the islands. When about two miles off the North Manitou Island harbor they turned around and backed up to about a half mile from the dock where they ran into the heavy, solid ice. Here they proceeded to unload the contents of the cars onto the ice where about twenty men from the island eagerly awaited the cargo that consisted of bailed hay, one barrel of kerosene, five barrel of salt, 16 bags of flour, two cartons of tobacco, three crates of eggs, three boxes of butter, four bags of sugar, and one case of malt. After dispatching these supplies, the A. A. No. 6 proceeded on her way to Frankfort after a delay of three hours and 40 minutes at the Island. During winters of heavy ice the only way the people on the island could contact the mainland was through the carferries.

Launching of Wabash at Toledo

Wednesday June 22, 1927, Crew for Steamer Wabash arrived aboard in Toledo at 6:00 p.m. The Wabash was equipped with a gyro compass when she came out.

Thursday June 23rd all hands tuned to and she departed Toledo ship yards for trial run at 11:00 a.m. Ran over to Detroit River Main light and returned to tie up at the dock in ship yard at Toledo at 5:00 p.m. everything okay.

June 24th getting ready for sea.

June 25th Left Toledo ship yard at 11:45 a.m. arrived Detroit 5:00 p.m. and arrived St. Claire Light vessel 7:20 p.m.

June 26th arrived Lake Huron Lt. Vess at 1:10 a.m. steering 1 Gyro Harbor Beach 6:01 a.m., Thunder Bay Isle 12:20 P.M., Presque Isle 2:16 p.m. Instead of going through the regular Poe Reef Passage she steered for Spectacle Reef arrived abreast of there at 5:28 p. m. then Round Isle Passage arrived at Mackinaw Isle and stopped there at 7:00 p.m. and stayed 10 minutes. Full speed again at 7:10 p.m. arrived Mackinaw Point light at Mackinaw 7:40 p.m. White Shoal at 9:13 p.m. and Lansing Shoal Light Vessel 10:50 p.m. and instead of heading for Death Door Passage. Arrived at Pilot Isle 5:15 a.m. and Plum Isle 5:27 a.m. and abreast of Chambers Isle at 7:11 a.m. Arrived Menominee at 8:10 a.m. the A. A. No. 5 ahead, tied up at pier 8:25 a.m. tied up in slip at 10:00 a.m. and as rails did not fit, left slip at 10:30 a.m. and headed for the Soo Slip in Manitowoc. Arriving Manitowoc at 5:08 p.m. arriving Soo slip at 5:55 p.m.

Shipyard crew started to work burning rails to fit and fix blocks on apron pocket, so apron would fit. Engine arrived 11:25 p.m. and started to load. 5 hour 15 minute delay because ship yard crew working on stern. Left slip at 12:40 a.m. June 28, 1927.

Wabash leaving Manitowoc.

The Wabash departed Manitowoc at 1:01 a.m.. steering 63 gyro wind south, Light and clear. Arrived Frankfort 6:45 a.m. West slip 7:00 a.m. and engine unloaded at 7:45 a.m. Left slip after fueling. No cargo at 9:10 a.m. cleared breakwater at 9:37 a.m. bound for Charlevoix, Michigan. Arrived Charlevoix 3:03 p.m. tied up at 3:45 p.m. Left dock 5:50 p.m. departed Charelvoix 6:02 p.m. heading back to Frankfort.

Trip 855 Mon. Nov. 14, 1927--Dept. Frkt 8:00 a.m. Wind NE fresh rain and sleet, course N 5/8 E. Ck. down at 3:40 a.m. Proceeding under ck. and sounding by hand. 24 fathoms at 4:00 p.m. 19 fathoms at 4:20 p m. and 14 fathoms at 4:45 p.m. Working in slowly and picked up sound of fog whistle at 6:00 p.m. Arrived Manistique breakwater at 6:30 p.m.

It was trips like this made during thick, sub-zero weather, when the old hand lead was the only known method to ascertain the nearness of land, that made men at sea realize what a friend they found in the coming of our present day direction finders, which have practically eliminated the use of a hand lead.

Arrived Frankfort June 29, 1927 for regular trade and arriving there at 12:10 a.m. east slip 12:30 a.m. and made trip number 3 to Menominee, Michigan.

Wabash fire drill

Sunday, June 23, 1929, the A. A. No. 7 moored at the city dock in Kewaunee and took aboard 259 passengers for an excursion on Lake Michigan. They departed Kewaunee breakwater at 8:55 a. cruised north up the west shore and entered the Sturgeon bay canal into Green bay, passing through the bridges separating Sawyer and Sturgeon Bay. Thence westward to Sherwood Point and north around upper door county and outside into Lake Michigan through the notorious Death Door Passage. Thence south again, arriving at Kewaunee once more at 9:30 p.m. Thus ending one of the most picturesque trips on fresh water, covering a territory of much early historical interest while circumnavigating the upper half of Door county.

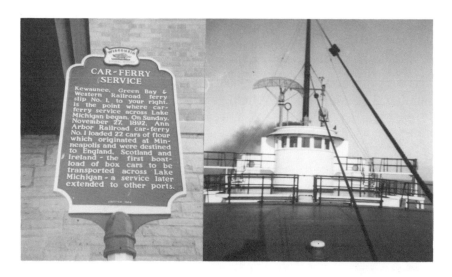

Wabash showing radar, direction finder anemometer for weather, loop antenna for direction finder, radar screen for radar and Historical Marker in Kewaunee.

Wabash on bottom in Frankfort harbor and the A. A. No. 5 removing cargo.

Wabash in shipyard at Sturgeon Bay for annual inspection when Manitowoc shipyard was on strike. the A. A. No. 7 departed Kewaunee, Wisconsin at 12:50 p.m. on Sunday, July 27, 1929 with the wind northwest moderate and clear, steering E 5/8 N. shortly after clearing the breakwater a schooner hove into sight on the left bow. Coming closer and with the aid of the glass she was found to be the Lucia A. simpson hailing out of Milwaukee in ballast with distress signals floating aloft.

After looking her over while passing at reduced speed with her close aboard on the port side, the A. A. No. 7 came about, passed her a hawser and proceeded to tow her to Kewaunee. Here the Coast Guard came outside with their cutter and assisted the disabled schooner safely into the protection of the harbor.

The schooner L. A. Simpson was one of the last of the great white winged fleet of sailing ships, some of which, in the day s old could be seen in every port on the Great Lakes. She was built at Manitowoc in 1875 of wood, with a gross tonnage of 227 tons. In her prime she was recognized as one of the fastest three stickers afloat and had been often logged at 16 mi. per hr. with a fair wind. But in her present condition with all her canvas flying, about 8 or 10 miles was the best they could squeeze out of her.

The Simpson had recently been purchased by the Northern Marine Co. of Milwaukee. After they had made several changes aboard and equipped her with salvage and deep sea diving equipment she put to sea with expectation of hunting sunken treasure from some of the many hulls still resting peacefully on the bottom of the Great Lakes.

Having been towed outside by a tug the schooner Simpson departed the Milwaukee breakwater on the morning of July 26, 1929. After hauling in her tow line she squared away to the northward under a full spread of canvas, running before a fair wind out of the southwest.

The wind held in her favor all day and she made good time beating it up the west shore.

Late that night the wind shifted to the northward coming over the starboard bow. Captain Simenson, rather than tack and get too far away from land and as the glass was falling, decided to come about and seek anchorage under the lee of Twin River Point until weather conditions improved.

Shortly after they came around and when about twelve miles off Algoma she was struck with a sudden squall that tore out of the northwest like a living gale forcing her to heel over on her beam ends with lee rail awash and snapped off the mizzen mast at the cross trees. The jerking movement while righting herself to an even keel caused a second break in the spar just above the after cabin. Another gust of wind carried the big stick overboard on the port side, the dragging of which caused a dangerous list in the ship.

Jumping into the mist of torn rigging the crew succeeded in chopping away the stays that cleared the wreckage by setting the mast, shrouds, sails and rigging free to float away in the open sea.

Thus she was disabled by the loss of her mizzen and shipping water through reopened seams in her wooden hull, caused by the stress and strain while climbing over the monstrous seas as they broke along her side at unaccustomed angeles from the loss of weight and buoyancy of her after mast. With wooden hulls considered old at 30 years, it's just a miracle that she rode out the storm.

With a wonderful display of seamanship Captain Simenson at the helm gradually worked her in under the lee of the land, while the entire crew shortened sail and manned the hand pumps.

Although the water gained steadily in her hold, where a depth of five feet was sounded at the time help arrived, she managed to stay afloat.

With the coming of dawn a distress signal, the American flag inverted and flying at half mast, was raised aloft. It was in this condition that the A. A. No. 7 found her later in the day and towed her to Kewaunee.

The following day, after docking in Kewaunee, the crew succeeded in caulking her seams and thus stopping the leaks. Later a tug arrived and towed her to the ship yards in Sturgeon Bay, Wisconsin. Here she had expectations of undergoing extensive repairs, but later it was decided by the owner that this expense would be to great.

After her salvage machinery was removed, she was towed to her final resting place on the beach and dismantled. So after 54 years of faithful service (most of which was spent on Lake Michigan through fair weather and foul alike) this once proud ship of the sea, like many others of her kind, that played such a so easily forgotten and very important historical part in the building of commerce, etc., on our inland seas, came to rest in the boneyard of Sturgeon Bay. There she burned during the big fire which also destroyed the E.G. Crosby, Petoskey, Kenosha, Waukegon and many other on December 3, 1935.

Lucia Simpson

First mention of direction finder--November 20, 1929.

The A. A. No. 7 left Manitowoc at 10:50 a.m. wind N.E. gale with rain. Course N.E. by E ½ E. The wind reached gale force shortly after they left and soon the seas became larger and larger. When she was about one hour out the A. A. No. 7 met three monstrous seas coming along together and as she dipped her stem into the trough of the first one the second sea came aboard and stove in some of her cabin windows. This, of course, took the way off her and she refused to look in the third sea, coming around by herself against her helm.

Captain Larson, then her master, headed her back for Manitowoc where she laid wind bound until 6:00 a.m. on October 23rd. there was still a big sea running when she left, but the wind had let up considerably. This is the same blow that sank the Grand Trunk carferry Milwaukee with all hands aboard about 90 miles farther south.

November 14, 1929 Trip 845 5:30 p.m. The Wabash

departed Kewaunee. Big south sea in lake. November 15, 2:15 a.m. Nose on beach at South Manitou Isle, left at 6:00 a.m. arriving Frankfort 8:45 a.m.

December 18, 1929 Departed Menominee 5:05 p.m. wind N.E. gale snow. Stuck in ice at 6:25 p.m. The A. A. No. 6 arrived at 1:05 a.m. December 20th and she also became stuck in the ice. the A. A. No. 5 arrived at noon on December 20th. the A. A. No.s 5 and 6 worked on Wabash and released her at 3:00 a.m. December 21st. The A. A. No.s 5 and Wabash stuck side by side at 11:00 a.m. and the Wabash released again at 5:15 p.m. December 21 and arrived at Sherwood Point at 6:15 p.m. and at Frankfort at 10:40 p.m.

On April 1st Departed Frankfort 11:30 a.m. North gale snow, big sea coming over sea gate after squaring away for canal and bent sea gate and damaged auto on stern arrived canal 6:30 p.m.

March 25, 1930 The Wabash departed Manistique 12:45 a.m. wind N.E. fresh, cloudy, course south on leaving received message on wireless, stating mail boat and Coast Guard boat both stuck in ice abreast of N. Manitou Isle and in need of assistance. Hauled S. E. at 4:25 a.m. checked slow at 4:30 waiting daylight full speed at 4:50 a.m. end of South Isle. Hauled east and reached boat at 6:45 a.m. 8 men taken aboard and fed at 6:45 Boats released and under way at 8:55 a.m. Arriving Frankfort 11:24. a.m. 4 hours and 40 minutes enroute releasing boats.

April 15th While going up Manitowocc river to dry dock rubbed the parked steamer Theo Roosevelt and damaged her upped works forward.

November 23rd The Wabash, arrived Frankfort and attempting to get into the slip Steamer was blown away from her moorings and broadside across Betsie Lake on to the bottom. It took several hours to release her with assistance of Tug Fred Gruling (about 3 hours) During this time with heavy working of engines in attempt to release steamer propeller wheels struck hard on some sunken obstacles either logs or bottom. Possible damage to wheels and shaft. Wabash rudder stock was bent and steering engine badly broken up in parts due to the grounding. Damage was done to the Tug Satisfaction-owned by Gruling Engineering Works of Green Bay, Wisconsin. Some dock damage to Rodal Fish Co. also clumps of 14 pilings belonging to the N. Michigan Co. were damaged and misplaced.

Sunday, June 14, 1931. First mention of finding harbor in fog without the use of hand lead depending solely upon the Radio Direction Finder. Also all sea gates were built higher in 1931.

On Wednesday, August 19, 1930 the A. A. No. 7 towed the disabled Tug Greling from Frankfort to Manitowoc shipyards. After parting the tow line twice she was two hours and forty minutes late enroute.

At 9:00 a.m. the men on watch in the pilot house noticed a life boat floating partly submerged about a point on the starboard bow. They checked down and called the captain who maneuvered the A. A. No. 7 around into position, with the life boat under her stern. They were then in midlake.

When coming closer they could se that it was the No. 1 life boat from the Steamer Buckeye state and of 180 cubic feet with a carrying capacity of 18 persons also that some of her air tanks were adrift. Seeing the life boat to be in fair condition, they decided to take it along. The best way to do this was to hoist it aboard as towing would cause much delay. Bay making both ends of the life boat fast to the partly raised sea gate and with the aid of the tow after capstans they picked up the boat and swung her inboard upon the spacious fantail stern of the A. A. No. 7's car deck.

The Purser of the A. A. No. 7 at orders from Captain Larson, wired the Coast Guard and they came out of Two Rivers and took charge of the boat. After picking up the life boat 7 cruised around that area for about one hour seeking other wreckage flotsam not aware of just what happened to the mother ship. It was later found out that Steamer Buckeye State had lost her No. 1 the A. A. No. while diving into the teeth of a north east gale the day before.

On Friday, February 10, 1933 the A. A. No. 7, approaching the Frankfort breakwater and while running before a big southwest sea and wind with everything on her wide open, hit the slush ice just outside at 5:35 a.m.

The A. A. No. 6 was then stuck fast in the ice at the outside end of the inner piers partly blocking the channel. When the A. A. No. 7 with most of her way gone from forcing herself through this heavy ice maneuvered around the A. A. No. 6 her starboard wheel stuck some submerged object and broke off. She was then abreast of the inside light. Still having some headway, she fought her way into the harbor with the remaining propeller. The Steamer Wabash acting as a tug assisted her into the slip, docking at 5:00 p.m. Here she unloaded her cargo and took on fuel and supplies for the long expected stay at the ship yards at Manitowoc.

Although these carferries have been known to make better than half speed with only one wheel and work around a harbor much faster than one would expect (on one occasion the A. A. No. 7 was only 20 minutes late to Manitowoc with only one wheel in operation), the Marine Superintendent O. T. Larson after talking it over with both captains and realizing that it was in the dead of winter decided it best to have the Wabash assist the A. A. No. 7 in her crippled condition to Manitowoc.

Just after diner Sunday February 12th the wind became puffy and started to die out. at 1:00 p.m. the same afternoon the Wabash backed down to the bow of the A. A. No. 7. After making her steel towing cable fast to the A. A. No. 7 she proceeded to tow her outside. Creeping slowly through the ice packed channel they departed the Frankfort breakwater at 2:30 p.m. The wind was south, fresh and clear. They steered south by west.

When they were underway for about one hour the wind breezed up from the southwest and started a big sea running. At 4:00 p.m. she was not towing very well and when abreast of

Manistee at 4:40 p.m. the A. A. No. 7 dipped her bow down into the trough of a big sea and the next sea struck her with such force that it parted the tow line between the towing post (timberhead) and the chalk in the bulwarks on the bow. Knowing that it was useless to try and make this tow line fast again, in such a seaway Captain Larson headed the A. A. No. 7 into the sea steering southwest at 4:45 p.m..

In her disabled condition she could not look into this howling gale and monstrous sea very long and at 5:00 p.m. rolling heavily she came around by herself with the sea, and easing her off before it they steered north northwest in an effort to stay outside the slush ice that then extended about six miles off the beach.

With weather and ice conditions such as they were the A. A. No. 7 decided to make a try for shelter at the home port of Frankfort. So at 5:45 p.m. they steered north northeast heading on the radio beacon at Point Betsie, just north of Frankfort. At 7:00 p.m. with the one engine doing her very best and with that big southwest sea and gale of wind driving her along they hauled her in and headed for the harbor entrance.

Shortly after entering the slush ice outside she lost her headway. Coming to a dead stop at 7:30 p.m. she stuck fast in the ice that was slowly moving along with wind and sea bodily carrying the A. A. No. 7 to the northward, past the harbor and closer to the shallow water of the beach.

Being at the mercy of the elements the A. A. No. 7 swung around, heading southwest and wallowed around almost dipping her rails under in the trough of the ice covered seas. (Note: By sea faring men of the seven seas it is understood that no ship rolls as deep as a carferry in a big sea, covered with slush ice.) This rolling was soon overcome by dropping both anchors and partly settling her by pumping about 12 feet of water in Number 1, 2 and 4 holds. She stopped drifting then and none too soon as a sounding showed on 20 feet of water under her keel. Soon ice started making outside her, forming a bumper against the deep swells

130

rolling in from seaward and she quieted down for the night.

The Wabash was also helpless in this terrific southwest gale and sea, and she after entering the ice, became fast and drifted down almost to the A. A. No. 7 and nearly on the beach. The A. A. No. 3 hove into sight from the west shore at 9:30 p.m. and after looking over the conditions here squared away to the northward, heading for the shelter of Manitou Isle and there awaited a shift of wind.

At 3:00 a.m. the next morning, February 13th the wind shifted to the northward. This relieved the pressure on the ice surrounding the A. A. No. 7 and the Wabash and started knocking the top of the big seas rolling outside from the southward.

After pumping out the holds that shallowed her draft and broke her loose from that ice bound berth, they started working ahead on the one engine and heaving up the anchors that were well fast on the bottom and leading seaward. Slowly she started ahead and gained way as she gradually picked up chain, heading out to sea, clearing the ice at 5:25 a.m. With the wind then north light and clear, they started for Manitowoc on her regular course S.W. by W.

The Wabash cleared the ice about the same time, but as the weather had moderated the A. A. No. 7 needed no further assistance.

The A. A. No. 7 made excellent time across the lake and was abreast of Twin River Point at 10:40 a.m. and arrived at Manitowoc breakwater at 11:40 a.m. Here the Tug Pitz took her tow line and assisted her up the river to the Dry Dock. While the A. A. No. 7 was working into the dock her port wheel struck some submerged obstruction and broke off three of the four blades and cracked her shaft, thus arriving in the nick of time with no wheels at all. She docked at 4:50 p.m.. February 13 and was at sea again on February 18th.

On March 8, 1933, the A. A. No. 6 left Manitowocc at 10:05 p.m. with the wind northwest, strong, and clear steering northeast by E½E bound for Frankfort. As there was a large sea running, after passing Two River Point she held up to the northward all the way across the lake, and when nearing the east shore she squared away before the sea heading for the harbor. Approaching the harbor entrance she dipped her nose down between two monstrous seas and smelling the bottom refused to answer her helm properly. This cause her to drift down onto the rip rap off the north end of the south pier, fetching up on her starboard side just aft amidships, with a terrible grinding jar, at 6:00 a.m..

After her stern dragged clear of the bottom she swung back up to the windward and made the inner harbor. Arriving at the slip she unloaded and shifted out along side the dock to tie up for an examination of the hull, etc. Other than a broken sea cock and several dents in her bottom along the starboard side aft she seemed to be in seaworthy condition. To make sure they took her out into the harbor and ran her full speed ahead and full astern in the heavy ice. They could find nothing wrong. After tying up again they tipped her up so the ship's carpenter could repair the damaged sea cock.

When this was completed they hung on for weather about 12 hours and then left for the ship yards at Manitowoc. She left Frankfort at noon on March 10.

In crossing the lake she made her regular time and steered the same as usual. there were no new vibrations in her hull and she handled perfectly at sea and on her way up the Manitowoc River to the dry dock. Arriving there they found the following repairs necessary. Several bad indentations on the starboard side abreast the engine room, below the load line, plates damaged to keel from stern post to about 75 feet forward of seam, rudder bent and rudder frame broken near top of blade, rudder sleeve broken off at stern post, the starboard propeller had two broken blades and the starboard shaft was bent. They also found it necessary to refill the stern bearings and ship a new rudder. 16 plates were taken off and repaired, a new sea cock was put in on the starboard side. She was placed in operation again on March 18th.

It is interesting to note that ships at sea, regardless of shape, size or flag assist each other in every way whenever possible. In this case the government dredge, General Mead, took a head line for the A. A. No. 6 on January 7, 1933 and lifted her head up into the wind after she had drifted down onto a clay bank at the north side of the channel in the Manitowoc River. Without this friendly assistance she might have lain there until a shift of wind and done considerable damage to herself.

The A. A. No. 6 tied up for her annual inspection at the shipyards in Manitowoc on July 14, 1934. After inspeciton, she laid there until september 14. She fitted out and then left for Frankfort at 10:53 on the fourteenth. Steering NE by E ½ the weather was calm with a light rain. As this trip was on a weekend she had aboard most of the homeward bound crew of the A. A. No. 7. The A. A. No. 7 was then in the yards for inspection and minor repairs.

At 1:35 a.m. the next morning a light breeze sprang up from the eastward and it set in thick.

About 2:10 a.m. the look out on watch sang out from the foc'sle deck to the mate on the bridge that he heard a steamer blowing three whistles for fog, about 2 ½ points on the port bow. The mate, also hearing the steamer immediately stopped both engines, rang the bell for the captain, and blew the approaching steamer one blast of his whistle. This was promptly answered. the A. A. No. 6 then put her helm to the port and blew one blast again just as the captain entered the pilot house. The approaching steamer answered with three blasts, followed by the danger signal, just as her lights broke through the fog. The master of the A. A. No. 6 then rang for full speed ahead on the port engine in an effort to swing her clear and avoid a collision. At the same time he turned in the alarm bell for "all hands on deck." The ships collided at 2:15 a.m. with a heavy smashing sound. The A. A. No. 6 listed over, as in a seaway, as the other steamer stuck her bow into the port side abreast the after life boat. No damage was done below the water line.

.

133

Bow of the Leopold after collision with the A. A. No. 6

The A. A. No. 6 then backed up to render assistance, but the captain of the other ship, giving her name as the N.F. Leopold, sang out that they had but little damage and were in no need of any help. Both ships then proceeded on their way, the A. A. No. 6 arriving in Frankfort at 5:10 a.m.

The A. A. No. 6 went to the ship yards at Manitowoc the next trip where she received temporary repairs, being needed in service until freight slacked up. She returned to the yards on October 5 and had the dent made in her side by the Leopold taken out.

December 3, 1934 The Wabash arrived Manitowoc 4:38 a.m. C.N.W. slip 4:50 a.m. left slip 9:50 a.m. tied up at flour dock at 10:00 a.m. and arrived Soo slip at 2:25 p.m. (delay S.E. gale)When ready to leave Str. Canadoc was stuck on bottom in 10th Street Bridge and the Wabash started pulling on Str. Canadoc at 4:30 p.m. but was of no avail. December 5th the M.C. Mullen & Pitz equipment started lightening the Canodoc at 10:45 a.m.

December 6th the Str. Canadoc released at 10:15 a.m. and the Wabash left for C.N.W. slip and thence to Frankfort leaving Manitowoc at 10:15 p.m.

July 29, 1934 Arrived Kewaunee 6:05 p.m. coal boat unloading at the piers. We are advised by G. G. Tomlison S.S. Co. that the Wabash passed the Str. Siena while unloading at Kewaunee Grain Co. at such speed that the Siena was sucked away from the dock causing the boom of the Siena to damage a roof of building 1 loosen some piles on dock of grain Co.

April 14, 1935 Departed Kewaunee 7:15 p.m. bound lite for Menominee arrived canal 7:02 a.m. April 15th gale and snow outside. Arrived at bridge 7:45 a.m. but bridge tender was unable to open it on account frozen shut, so the Wabash had to turn around and go out in the lake and come back and then he had it open. N.W. gale snow. Departed canal 8:40 a.m. arrived canal again at 9:10 a.m. (2 hour 5 minutes account bridge frozen) Arrived Menominee 11:30 a.m. 11 hour 45 minute delay in lake account N.W. gale and snow.

Saturday, June 29, 1935 -- Trip 462 the A. A. No. 7 departed Manitowoc at 10:00 p.m. wind calm and clear. Course N.E. By E ½ E when just outside they noticed distress flares burning just off her course to the southward and backed down alongside finding it to be a small craft with motor trouble. The A. A. No. 7 wired into Manitowoc station and they relayed the distress call to Two River Coast Guard Station who hurriedly appeared on the scene. the A. A. No. 7 stood by until the Coast Guard arrived and then proceeded on her course losing thirty minutes of her running time.

August 31, 1936 Put new load line on midships; it became universal abut this time.

In 1937 when the state took over the A. A. No. 4 her name was changed the City of Cheboygan. She was painted white and the state took real good care of her. This is a nice sheltered run across here and she seldom operates during the bad winter weather.

135

The A. A. No. 4 after she was sold to State in 1937

The A. A. No. 4 renamed City of Cheboygan in slip at St. Ignace

First mention of new Bendix Sprinkling System in 1937.

November 27, 1937 Depart Kewaunee 2:25 p.m. wind S fresh, rain and fog. running ½ speed steered 9 minutes E by S then hauled S.E. and at 2:45 p.m. hauled S ¼ E for Manitowoc. Heard a steamer 1 point on right of starboard bow at 3:15 p.m. blowing 3 blasts and checked to slow speed at 3:17 p.m. and gave a signal of 2 blasts but received no answer, then blew 3 blasts and swung Wabash to left about 4 points and again gave 2 blasts and got no answer. Had right engine stopped and backed on left engine to swing. We then picked up the No. 22 coming down on us and again blew 2 blasts. When we saw P.M. 22 hauling to left we put the wheel and rudder to right and backed full astern on right engine and full ahead on left engine to try to swing stern clear of P.M. 22. The P.M 22 struck the Wabash a glancing blow about amidships on the starboard side at 3:23 p.m. Both engines stopped at 3:24 p.m. when we learned that both steamers were in safe condition, started up at 1/2 speed at 3:33 p.m. 4 frames and plating above car deck at gangway damaged on starboard side. twin River Point at 4:00 p.m. Hauled S.W. x S at 4:28 p.m. Hauled W at 5:00 p.m. checked slow at 5:14 p.m. arrived Manitowoc 5:19 p.m. did not repair this until inspection of next year. No delay.

Laid in Manitowoc during 1940 blow. Delayed 39 hours- wind S.W. gale, snow.

While the A.A. No. 6 was steering east from Manitowoc on October 2, 1919 with the wind blowing a gale from the south southeast and a dense fog, a steamer broke out of a fog bank close aboard on the starboard bow. In order to clear him they hauled to the northward on a hard left wheel. This brought her into the trough of the sea, rolling her rail almost under. Before they could get clear of the other ship enough to haul her back up to where she did not roll they dumped two cars of timbers over on the car deck which caused ten hours delay while unloading in Frankfort.

In February 1939, the A. A. No. 6 left Manistique at 2:30

a.m. on the seventeenth bound south for Frankfort. While on the way down the wind freshened up from the south southwest and soon made a big sea in the lake. Coming from almost ahead the A. A. No. 6 made good weather of it other than being three hours late.

The piers of Frankfort line up almost due east and west so it was necessary for her to run by the place far enough to the southward to get the wind and sea behind her when entering the harbor.

She had fetched high enough by 12:05 a.m. the next morning so the captain thinking he had found a smooth spot let her come around on a hard left wheel with both engines wide open. She was slow in coming and when about half way around laid over into the trough between two big seas with her lee rail almost awash and shook herself for and aft as the next seas struck under her quarter just before she straightened herself up and headed on the harbor lights.

While squaring away here she rolled three carloads of heavy copper billets out through the sides of the box-cars and onto her car deck. She also shifted the lumber in two gondola cars.

Arriving at the piers at 12:30 a.m. she became stuck fast in the slush ice that had been packed in by the westerly seas. She was delayed by the ice for 11 hours before she finally arrived inside. Once at the dock it took the section crew over 3 hours to reload the billets so that she should unload the cars and be ready for sea again.

Passed the last schooner ever to sail Lake Michigan going north past Frankfort, the Oliver H. Perry, at 5:20 a.m. on July 11, 1939

The Armistice Day storm of 1940 was the worst storm on the Great Lakes since the storm of 1913 when so many ships were lost.

At 11:10 a.m. on the 11th, the A. A. No. 6 left Manitowoc bound for Frankfort. The wind was blowing strong from the southeast and it was raining. Not being able to steer the regular course because of the sea, they held up steering E by S. At 1:00 p.m. they squared away for home and steered N E ½ E. One hour later the wind came around and blew a living gale out of the southwest.

The sea soon started to make and knowing that they could not enter the home port in this gale they hauled North at 2:30 p.m. and headed for the shelter of South Manitou Island. (Running with the sea was the only way in which any ship could live very long in a storm like this.)

While pounding northward, sea tossed and storm driven, past that inviting looking shore near Frankfort and Point Betsie, the wind blew so hard that it seemed to fairly lift the tops from the roaring, foaming seas, as they madly raced along, at times almost submerging her sides, and spray it an all directions at once.

The A. A. No. 6 passed Point Betsie at 5:50 p.m. when to make things worse it started to snow. Luckily they were able to make out the outline of the shore, through the falling snow an ever increasing darkness, far enough ahead to keep off the beach as they worked her around the east end of the island and into the lee.

She rounded the Island at 7:30 p.m. losing the sea the captain checked down and eased her nose up onto the sandy beach near the South Island harbor. The force of the wind was so great that they had to work both engines full ahead to keep her from going broadside on the beach.

At daybreak on the twelfth it was still snowing and blowing a gale which started to moderate around noon. the A. A. No. 6 laid there O.K. with her engines at half speed ahead. Early on the morning of the thirteenth the wind started to peter out and at 6 a.m. they decided to put to sea and head for home.

Backing at full speed astern she refused to leave the beach. The captain then ordered her cargo shifted aft and her after holds filled with water in an effort to tip her down by the stern enough to slide her off the bank on which her bow was resting. There was forty feet of water under her stern.

After they had tipped her back as far as possible the

139

engineers worked her astern with both engines wide open, but she still refused to budge. They then wired the office at Frankfort for assistance and the A. A. No. 3 arrived at 6 p.m..

The A. A. No. 3 hung off on her anchor, backed down to the stern of the A. A. No. 6 and after making fast the tow line started to pull at 6:15 p.m. With the A. A. No. 3 working ahead on the line and swinging the stern of the A. A. No. 6 slowly back and forth for about 30 degrees of the compass, by working her rudder hard over both ways, and while the A. A. No. 6 worked her engines full astern, the A. A. No. 6 slid off into deep water at 7 p.m.

They then hauled in their lines and with a parting salute of her whistle the A. A. No. 3 departed for Manistique and the A. A. No. 6 for Frankfort. She arrived there at 10 p.m. on November 13th.

The A. A. No. 7 departed Frankfort at 10:30 p.m. Saturday, April 10, 1948. The wind was south, strong and cloudy. Steering 283 bound for Sturgeon Bay canal just 53 miles away, enroute to Menominee, Michigan. She had a short cargo of seven loaded freight cars, three empty ones and three autos.

As the wind was blowing hard with a fair size sea running and growing larger, this light cargo required a change of course to the windward, or holding up, in order to make a decent run across the lake. After they had held up enough they squared away from the canal with the wind and sea behind her steering 325 . Thus being 11° higher than the canal line up for drift.

It had been raining since midnight with occasional lightening which made the visability poor and also filled the atmosphere with static thus rendering the radio direction finder almost useless. So with the wind and sea driving her along before this blinding rain storm and even with the time lost in changing courses figured in, the A. A. No. 7 like many other ships before her, made much better time than expected at 4:22 a.m. April 11, just as the captain was about to check her down, she piled up on the sandy beach just south of the canal at fill speed coming to a

140

sliding stop without any list.

While the captain backed her wide open in effort to release her the first officer and lookout examined the bottom in all her holds finding no leaks nor damage of any kind. The watchman's soundings showed 12 feet of water under her stem, 11 feet amidships and 15 feet at her stern. Because the strong sea was breaking as it rolled under her stern and along her sides it was hard to get these sounding exact. While working the engines back and forth and also using her helm they found that she would swing 15 but would not go astern.

About 9:00 a. m. a small fish tug came sliding alongside with a radio phone aboard and relayed a message, describing the accident to Marine Superintendent Herring at Frankfort. He ordered tugs sent out at once from the Roen Wrecking Company at Sturgeon Bay. Two tugs arrived at 1:30 p.m. the Spuds and John Roen, III. After the towing bridle was adjusted, they started pulling and continued to pull all night with no results, although by pulling at various angles they could swing her about 20○.

The Wabash arrived at 6:15 a.m. on April 12, and after making fast the six inch hawser of the A. A. No. 7 to her stern timberhead she assisted the tugs in pulling. After parting the hawser twice the Wabash left the scene and continued on her way at 10:20 a.m..

The A. A. No. 5 arrived at 1:30 p.m., but did not take a line. While she was standing by at 2:00 p.m. the A. A. No. 7, with two tugs doing their very best started astern and after casting off the tow lines proceeded on her way to the canal at 2:25 p.m..

Captain H.B. Meno, our former Superintendent of Marine, who was assigned to the case as a marine surveyor came aboard on a tug and reported no damage after checking the A. A. No. 7 over from stem to gudgeon. The A. A. No. 7 in taking to the beach was very fortunate in picking that particular spot in which to park as it was the only sandy place for miles along that rock bound coast.

The A. A. No. 7 docked this same year in October and a

141

complete survey of her bottom showed no damage from this beaching at full speed. She fared much better than the dutch ship, Prince William, which after coming half way around the globe hit the beach during a dense fog almost in this same place and tore out $100,000 of her bottom.

The A. A. No. 5 and South Park

Looking east over Frankfort Harbor north arm of the breakwater and inside piers at harbor entrance. Carferry in slip on Elberta side and road leaving slip going around bay to Frankfort. The long street is Forest Avenue connecting with Highway 115 going east out of town 50 US 31. It crosses M22 on 7th Street at the east end of the city.

The Steamer C. E. Redfern, loaded with pulpwood, sank about two miles off Point Betsie at 11:15 p.m. Sunday night on September 19, 1937. After the Coast Guard cutters from Frankfort and South Manitou Isle had removed her 15 crew members. She was loaded with 500 cords of eight foot pine and spruce pulpwood and left Nahma, Michigan, in the upper peninsula late Saturday evening, bound for Manistee, Michigan, with her cargo consigned to the filer Fibre Co.

Shortly after midnight it breezed up from the northwest building up a sea. While the heavily loaded Redfern labored in this seaway she started making water in her holds. Soon her limbers became partly plugged with the fallen bark off the pulpwood making it impossible to keep her dry with the pumps, and she gradually started to fill up and slowly but surely submerge. About 2:00 a.m. she developed engine trouble and displayed her distress signals.

It was this signal that the A. A. No. 7 with Captain Chick Hanson in charge, picked up at 3:00 a.m. while steaming on her way north bound for Manistique, having left Frankfort at 1:00 a.m. the A. A. No. 7 immediately headed for her wide open and when within healing distance found it to be the motor ship Redfern with engine trouble, leaking badly with her cargo of pulpwood floating all around her and not having any power was rolling hard in the trough of the sea. the A. A. No. 7 opened her storm oil tanks, worked down close to her from the windward, and floated her 8-inch manila tow line down to her. After this was made fast she slowly towed the Redfern along before the wind where she rode the sea that much better. Meanwhile the A. A. No. 7 had wired in for the local Coast Guard.

At 6:30 a.m. the tow line parted from chafing across her stem. As the Coast Guard cutter was then in sight the A. A. No. 7 did not try to again make the tow line fast but kept up to the windward of the Redfern, thus making her lee water and she rode

143

along on that storm oiled covered sea in good shape until the cutter from South Manitou isle arrived and got a line on him at 7:30 a.m. the A. A. No. 7 stood by until the big Cutter Escanaba hove into sight at 8:30 a.m. and then proceeded on her way north after being delayed her for 7 hours.

The cutter from Frankfort took off all members of the Redfern crew without one of them getting wet except a watchman who was discovered aboard after the others had abandoned her. He had gone back to his room to pack his gear and along with Mr. Walmer, who was next to the last man off, were the only ones to save any of their personal belongings. Captain O.T. Olsen saved only a clean shirt and a few bills. His license, ship's papers and personal gear sank with the ship just five minutes after the watchman was taken off. A great deal of credit was given the Frankfort crew especially for their splendid seamanship.

Captain Olsen stated that there was no insurance on the boat, but that the cargo was insured. All the crew of fifteen hailed from Marinette, Wisconsin, except one who came from Marysville, Michigan.

She broke up and sank in 30 fathoms of water about two miles north west of Point Betsie at 10:05 a.m. Later part of her floating house was towed to Frankfort by Luedtke Engineering Company and their crane lifted it on the dock, but nothing of any value was found inside.

Members of her crew were taken to Frankfort, fed, and lodged, and most of them returned home the next day on the carferry for Menominee. For several trips afterwards the carferry ran into part of her floating pulpwood cargo.

The Steamer Redfern was 47 years old having been built by Davidson Ship yards at Bay City in 1890 for the Hines Lumber Company, who later sold her to Mr. Ross Wentworth, and he sold her to Captain Orin W. Angwall and Captain Olsen in 1931 for $7,500. She was 181 feet long and had a 35 foot beam and 680 gross tons. At the time of her sinking she was on her twenty-first trip of the season.

Redfern off Point Betsie 1938

The A. A. No. 7 on beach, Roen tug and John Roen

Edward H. Anderson tied to dock in Benton Harbor 1965
The A. A. No. 4 after her conversion to City of Cheboygan, then
sold to E. H. Anderson and renamed. She was used for a potato
boat at Washington Island

Kewaunee Harbor showing the A. A. No. 7 on her way in.
Remains of old wooden harbor piers still standing.

The Francisco Morazan driven on the S.W. end of south Manitou Isle before a south sea and snow on November 29, 1960. She can be seen from the decks of the Manistique bound ships, still standing straight, proud and tall as the day of her stranding and makes a pastime sight for tourists as the ships usually pass about 5 or 6 miles off. Several salvage attempts have been made but any profits or benefits remain entirely up to the kindness of wind and sea. Also souvenir hunters have about stripped her clean.

During the rebuilding of Boat 6, which started on in July of 1958. Boat 6 was not only cut in two and lengthened 34 feet, but she also was cut horizontally fore and aft above her whale-streak, raising the height of her car (freight) deck two feet.

This two-way enlargement increased her carrying capacity by an additional 1,200 tons and she was able to carry four additional freight cars of much greater height, including the new "piggy back' trailers and other odd freight carrier sizes.

Although several carferries have been lengthened in this manner, this is the first time one has ever been cut lengthwise to raise the deck.

Boat 6 was also repowered with twin Nordberg diesel engines of 2,500 horsepower each. She also was the first carferry to have controllable pitch propellers increasing maneuverability, besides many other modern improvements, including a new streamlined pilot house. Her two old smoke stacks were replaced by a single stack with a raked look. Speed was increased to about 18 miles per hour.

It was estimated by shipbuilding officials that the renovation project, costing $2.5 million, would save about three-fifths of the cost of a new carferry.

She was renamed Arthur K. Atkinson.

Picture #1

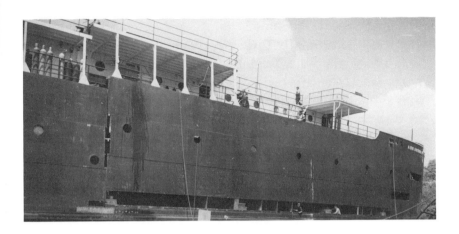

Picture #2

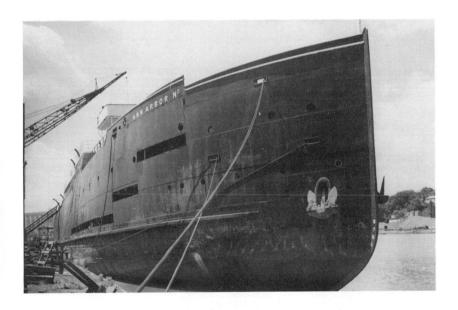

Picture #3
Picture 1 shows the A. A. No. No. 6 at the ship yards at
Manitowoc, Wisconsin. Showing how she was cut in two
athwartships and lengthened 34 feet. While she was high and dry
in the dry dock she was cut into, slid apart and a new section built

in the open space. Picture #2, the A. A. No. 6 at the ship yards being into horizontally fore and aft above the whales-streak-raising the height of her freight deck 2 ft. This was the first time for this kind of enlargement of carferries. Picture #3 The A. A. No. 6 showing the horizontal cut and raising the height of the freight deck.

The A. A. No. 6 rebuilt and renamed Arthur K. Atkinson

Wabash coated with ice going through railroad bridge at Sturgeon Bay coming east.

In 1962, while the merger with the D.T. & I. R.R. was pending, the "Wabash" spent four months in the yards of the Manitowoc Shipbuilding Co. where she underwent extensive remodeling and repairs. Her hull was sliced horizontally and the height of her entire cargo deck was raised 42 inches so that she now had the overhead clearance of 18 feet 11 inches which was necessary for the transportaion of piggy back and other lofty freight.

Her old-fashioned hand fired boilers were replaced with oil burners and her double stacks were replaced with a streamlined single stack carrying a new insigna, part of it, the cross carried on the insigna of all the D.T. & I. R.R. freight cars. Many other parts of the ship also were modernized.

It was not until August of 1962, after many delays, that the purchase of the Ann Arbor by the D.T. & I. was finally approved by the Interstate Commerce Commision. One of its first acts on taking over the railroad was to send the Wabash to Manitowoc for further modernization and repairs, and rename her.

Wabash being raised at shipyard at Manitowoc

[Left]Wabash out of yard and renamed City of Green Bay
[Right]City of Green Bay going through Sturgeon Bay canal left.
Taken from deck of Bay showing Str. Rocket at oil tanks and
dredge Hains coming into harbor.

The Susie Q hit off Two River by the A. A. No. 7

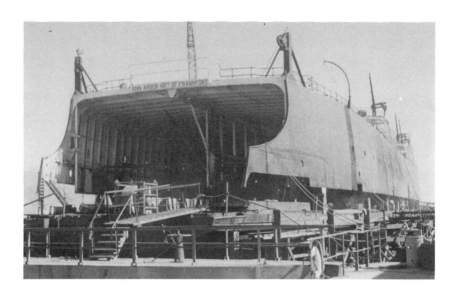

Picture #1

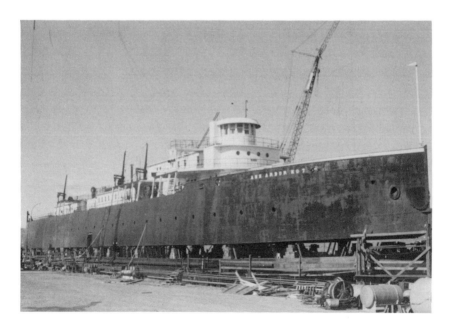

Picture #2

Picture #3

Picture #1 the A. A. No. 7 in dry dock being raised. Picture #2 the A. A. No. 7 in drydock showing stacks, lifeboats, etc. taken off. Picture #3 the A. A. No. 7 complete except for painting being towed out of dock by tug Sid Germander. Left Columbia boat Joseph Franz that later was taken to Sturgeon Bay for rebuilding.

A. A. No. 7 rebuilt and renamed Viking in Manitowoc Harbor on her first trip.

The Ann Arbor Number 5, was sold by the Ann Arbor Railroad to a west coast combine and then resold to a third owner and finally came into the Maritime Commission's possession in a subsidy trade. The Maritime Commission in turn sold her to the Bultema Dock and dredge Co. of Muskegon. She was then taken to the Bultema yards at Manistee.

On Thursday June 13, 1974 old friends bid a fond farewell to the "City of Green Bay". She had been sold to the Marine Salvage Company who were planning to tow her to Spain where she would be scraped.

A sad "Viking" bade farwell to the Frankfort harbor on May 16, 1983. She had been sold to Peterson Builders, Inc. of Sturgeon Bay, Wisconsin. Like a sad lady left to the fate that others would bestow upon her, she was towed out of the harbor and across the lake to await her fate.

On Wednesday, April 25, 1984, people watched as the Arthur K. Atkinson the last of the original Ann Arbor carferry fleet was towed out of the harbor and across the lake to Sturgeon Bay, Wisconsin, by the new owners Peterson Builders, Inc. It was a sad day for many as an era came to an end.

Advisor Photo

Picture of AKA as she was towed out of the Frankfort Harbor. in 1982.

"Where do ships go when they die, Granpa?" the small boy tugged at the coat tail of the old man standing at Lake Michigan's water edge.

"Wal now, that's a good question, Sonny. some of 'em sleep on the bottom. Others end up in scrap. Then again, some of 'em hardly ever die," the aged sailor mused as he focused tired eyes on a the Arthur K. Atkinson leaving the breakwater.

We wish to thank all those who contributed to this book. Especially all the men and women who served on the carferries and were a part of our heritage.

We wish to thank the following for their help in assembling the data and pictures for this book:

Bob Askevold
W.C. Bacon
Al Barnes
John Berger
C. D. Bishop
Allen Blacklock
Les Borst
Irma Brick
Francis Carter
Gust Carlson
Robert Classens
Roy Collins
Daryl Cornick
Roy Daley
Rev. E. J. Dowling S.J.
Edward C. Ericksen
J. H. Ferris
A. E. Frederickson
C. G. Frederickson
Charles O. Frederickson
Ed Gabrielson
Gust Gabrielson
Larry Geiger
Elsie Gilbert
Ole Glarum
David Glick
E. J. Gorman
J. F. Gregorski
Frank Hamilton
Dayton Hardy
Chan Harris
James Hawkins
Rose Hawley
C. L. Herring
George Honald
Andy Houston
Ralph Jackson
A. B. Jacobsen
Carl Jacobsen
Elliott Jacobsen
Pete Jeffs
Tony Jessen
Gilbert Johnson
Irma Johnson
Paul Kirby
F. A. Kolbeck
Charles LaFreniere
L. P. Larson
Carl Lints
Ferris McKessen

H. B. Meno
Jacob Nelson
J. E. Nelson
Vern Nobel
Lloyd Olson
Evelyn Perry
Joe Perry
Ellsworth Peterson
John Peterson
Dan Rathsack
E. F. Reich
John Roen
Magnor Roen
Peter Rokstad
Rev. St. Clair
Janet Coe Sanborn
James Sawtelle
Ray Schaffer
J. E. Schlosser
C. O. Slyfield
Ken Smith
C. T. Stoner
Douglas Stubbs
Fay Temby
Mable Temby
Roy Valitchka
George Vargo
R. T. Venn
Gerald Vigland
George Waters
George Watson
John Webber
R. G. Westfall
R. A. Winkel
Benzie County Patriot
Door County Advocate
Edwards Hardware
Great Lakes Historical   Society
Great Lakes Maritime   Institue
Kewaunee Enterprise
Manistee Public Library
Manitowoc Herald Times
Manitowoc Shipbuilding   Company
Marine Historical Society of
Detroit
Edwin Wilson Studio
Benzie Advisor

To Order additional copies of Frederickson's History of the Ann Arbor Train and Auto Ferries, please complete this form and return to Gulls Nest Publishing for quick shipment.

	Quantity	Price	Total
Ann Arbor Train and Auto Ferries	_____ X	$9.95 =	_____

Total   _____

Shipping & Handling
Please add $1.50 for each book
$ .75 for each additional book   _____

Michigan residents add 6% sales tax   _____

Total   _____

Name_____

Address_____

City_____State_____Zip_____

_____Payment enclosed

Send completed order form with check or money order to:

Gulls Nest Publishing
P.O. Box 272
Frankfort, MI   49635